THIS BOOK BELONGS TO:

....

....

Rebel Girls, Inc.
421 Elm Ave.
Larkspur, CA 94939
www.rebelgirls.com

Author: Nona Willis Aronowitz
Illustrator: Caribay Marquina
Art director: Giulia Flamini
Graphic designer: Kristen Brittain
Editor: Jess Harriton
Panel of Experts: Alexandra Vaccaro M.A., L.A.C.; Aline Topjian; Beth Lucas; Nicole Sparks, M.D.
Special Thanks: Eliza Kirby, Grace Srinivasiah, Jes Wolfe, Sarah Parvis, and Marina Asenjo

Printed in Italy
First Edition: May 2023
10 9 8 7 6 5 4 3 2 1
ISBN: 9781953424457
LCCN: 2022951878

CONTENTS

Chapter 5:
I Can Make the World a Better Place

INTRODUCTION

Hi there, Rebels!

Welcome to *Growing Up Powerful*! We're so glad you're here. You might know Rebel Girls from our Good Night Stories series or our podcast. Maybe you even have a favorite Rebel Girl—someone whose story you've read or listened to a bajillion times, someone you aspire to be like. We've loved sharing the inspiring tales of successful women around the world. And now we're starting a new, exciting chapter in our story.

With this book, we're turning our focus to another super amazing, talented, curious Rebel Girl who has a big heart and even bigger dreams. Can you guess who it is? The answer is . . . YOU! That's right, the book you hold in your hands is all about you and your best friend and your sister and your cousin and . . . well, you get the idea! *Growing Up Powerful* was created for this exact time in your life—the time when you're growing and learning and becoming your brilliant, kind, brave self!

This time in your life will come with some challenges that may test your confidence. In fact, we know that between the ages of 8 and 14, girls report feeling a big drop in their confidence. And we're not okay with that. So we got together with a group of

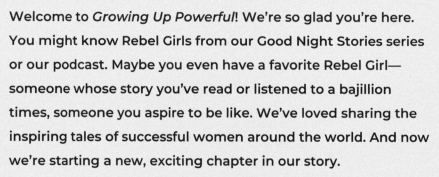

amazing Rebel Girls, led by our author Nona Willis Aronowitz, to help you navigate this important time, while keeping your confidence as strong as ever. Think of this book as a how-to manual for this chapter (pun intended!) in your life. We'll answer your questions and share our wisdom and advice. Together, we'll navigate all the ups and downs of puberty and middle school with curiosity and joy.

What do you think of when you hear the phrase "growing up"? Maybe you think about starting a new school or making friends. Perhaps you think about your body changing or having more responsibilities at home. Maybe your mind goes to all the ways you can help out in your community as you become more independent. Perhaps there are excited butterflies fluttering in your stomach, or maybe it is more of an I'm-about-to-lose-my-lunch sort of feeling. Luckily, whatever you're thinking of and however you're feeling, we've got you covered.

Are you stressed about how much homework you suddenly have? Chapter 1 is all about how your mind works. It includes tons of tricks and tips for managing your workload and keeping your cool. Curious about getting your first period? Turn to page 98, and we'll walk you through everything you need to know. Want to get closer with your friends? Head to Chapter 3 for a fun friendship Q&A activity. Not sure how to strike up a conversation with someone at your new school? Skip to Chapter 4 for a run-through of exactly what to say to someone you'd like to be friends with. Trying to figure out how to jump-start an idea you have for a community project? We'll get to that in Chapter 5! Whatever you're going through and whatever questions you have, we've been there, and we're here to help.

In addition to all the great advice we've got for you, fun quizzes in every chapter will help you find the right type of exercise for you, discover what your next family activity should be, uncover your superpower, and more! Throughout this book, you'll also see stories and quotes from Rebels you admire, as well as notes from girls around the world who are experiencing the very same things you are. Plus, at the end of every chapter, our team of experts answers thoughtful questions submitted by our amazing readers and listeners around the world.

We know that growing up can be overwhelming at times. But it's also pretty amazing. As your body grows

bigger and stronger and your mind expands, more and more incredible opportunities to show your talents and strengths will come your way. We feel so lucky to be here for you during this incredible time in your life and to celebrate with you as you reach all the exciting milestones that come with growing up POWERFUL!

Stay Rebel!

The Rebel Girls Team

Download the Rebel Girls app to listen to meditations, exercises, stories from girls just like you, and conversations with our experts.

Whenever you come across a QR code, scan it, and you'll learn more about many of the topics in this book.

CHAPTER 1

My Brain Is Powerful

My brain is incredible.

It's buzzing with thoughts, ideas, and big dreams. It allows me to do all sorts of things, from cartwheels to math to memorizing all the lyrics to my favorite songs to imagining stories in faraway lands. My brain is also in control of my feelings, from a spark of anger to those warm-and-fuzzies. It's still forming—which is cool, but it can also be super confusing! But knowledge is power, right? So learning about how my brain works can help me understand, decode, and navigate the world.

YOUR BRAIN ON THE MOVE

Right now, you're learning and growing so much—and that's in large part thanks to your brain. The changes your brain is going through will sometimes make you feel great, like when that tricky concept in algebra class finally makes sense and you feel that *click* of understanding. But other times the changes going on inside your head might not feel fantastic, like when your sister stains your favorite sweater and all of a sudden you feel your emotions go into overdrive. Understanding why these things happen is super empowering. Let's get into it!

That mushy, gray lump in your head develops in spurts—and these years, the ones you're living right now, happen to be some big ones for your brain. Your brain is actually being "rewired," adjusting to a new phase of your life. Two parts that are working incredibly hard right now? The **amygdala** and the **prefrontal cortex**.

The amygdala is in the middle of the brain, and it's in charge of BIG, sometimes scary emotions: fear, worry, sadness, joy. It's also the part of the brain that sends signals about what to do in a stressful or dangerous situation. (Scientists call this our "fight or flight" response, also known as a "gut feeling.") Your amygdala is maturing,

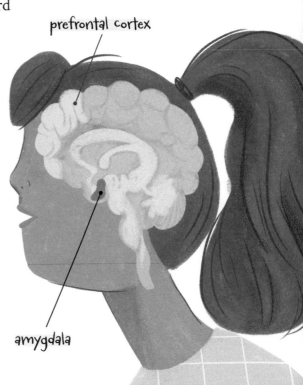

prefrontal cortex

amygdala

15

but it's not quite done, which means it might be hard to regulate all those emotions right now. That sudden feeling like you want to burst into tears? The moment when your mood goes from happy and content to bummer city? Believe it or not, that's your brain developing.

So what is the prefrontal cortex up to? It's all the way in the front of our brains, and it helps us make decisions, plan our days, and think through situations carefully. It's the place that tells you to do your science homework even though, *ugh*, all you wanna do is keep chatting with your bestie.

Brains don't put the finishing touches on the prefrontal cortex for many years—not until we're 25 years old.

Before then, you might make mistakes and iffy choices that you wish you hadn't made. That's okay. Learning from those moments is part of growing up.

Where Does All the Info Go?

There's *a lot* of information coming at our brains at
any given time, from teachers and families and
friends and phones and TVs . . . whew! How
do our brains possibly process it all? Well,
first of all, research shows that adult brains
and kid brains do this differently. Adults
mostly process information through the
prefrontal cortex, while preteens and teens
process information more through the amygdala.
And remember how the amygdala rules those great
big emotions? That's why you might find yourself *feeling*, not thinking,
when you decide to ride your bike without a helmet or scream at your sister
for barging into your room.

Some days, your brain might let you take a pause and think: *How will
this affect me in an hour, in a day, next year?* Other days, it'll be really
hard stop yourself from reacting to the moment you're in. And whether
you're a kid or an adult, different sides of your brain are responsible for
different things. Our brains are divided by two hemispheres: the right side
and the left side. The right controls our more creative, free-spirited side,
while the left handles logic and words. There's a myth that some people are
"right-brained," while others are "left-brained." It's fun to think that our
personalities come from one side or the other. But the truth is, everyone uses
both sides of their brain. They're constantly working together, no matter
what kind of person you are!

We Don't All Learn the Same

Our brains have the same basic parts, but they work in their own special ways.

Some people learn best when they see things. The imaginations of **eye-learners** are usually top-notch, and they might think in pictures rather than words.

Others absorb knowledge best when they use their ears. Do you store up facts when you overhear conversations? Do you sound out words or raise your hand a lot in class? You might be a **listener-learner**.

Then there are the **bookworms**: people who learn well through reading and writing. Bookworms love to curl up with a good story, take notes during class, and keep a diary. When you're thinking, words might show up in your brain rather than pictures.

There are also people who learn through touch and moving around. This style has a fun, fancy name: **kinesthetic**. If Legos have been your favorite toys since preschool or if you've always loved the sticky, scratchy, blobby sensations of arts and crafts, it's possible your brain works best when your hands are involved.

And, of course, many of us combine these learning styles. There's lots of amazing stuff to see and touch and read and do.

Letting Your Imagination Run Wild

Brains aren't just for learning—they're also for creating. It's great for your brain to exercise its artistic side, also known as the right side of your brain. The way you learn might tell you a little bit about how to be creative. Listener-learners often love music. Bookworms could become great poets and novelists. Creativity isn't just about the arts, either. Daydreaming, brainstorming, and problem-solving (all left-brained activities, by the way) count as creativity too. More good news? All those strong emotions coming through your amygdala will only help you be *more* creative as you start to experience the intensity of life. Your brain is lighting up in all kinds of places, every day. It can be exhausting, but it's also incredibly fun.

BEING HEALTHY INCLUDES YOUR MIND TOO

What does it mean when someone says "healthy" to you? You may think of fruits and vegetables, fresh air, and sunshine. A healthy body feels strong. And when you're not healthy, you rest, or you have some chicken soup, or you take some medicine.

Guess what? Our minds work in much the same way.

Just as it's important to keep your body healthy, your mind needs to be taken care of too. Being mentally healthy doesn't mean you're happy all the time. It just means you have ways to cope and soothe yourself when the going gets rough. You can see outside your own life and problems so you can be a good friend, sibling, and community member. You don't have trouble feeling great when something good happens—when you ace a test, let's say, or your favorite aunt comes to town.

Ideally, you'd always feel relaxed and happy, but like your body, your mind isn't always in tip-top shape. Think of it this way: if you twist your ankle and it swells up, you have to rest it, put ice on it, and take ibuprofen to feel better and reduce the swelling. Well, don't forget, our brains are body parts too. And sometimes they can feel under the weather or injured and need rest or even medicine. When we have mental-health issues, it doesn't mean we did anything wrong—we just need to figure out what the issue is and give our brains what they need to heal.

Your Brain Is a Muscle

When we want to make our bodies stronger, we know we have to lift weights or jump rope or play soccer. It's the same with our brains. We have to work them out to help them grow to be as powerful as they can possibly be. Every time we challenge our brains to do something new, it's like jumping jacks . . . for our mind!

Here are some ways to exercise your brain.

Read

The absolute best way to learn new words and fresh ways of expressing ourselves is to read, read, read. Books, poems, articles, even song lyrics—they all teach us distinct ways to communicate. There's lot of stimulation around you, and reading takes more focus than, say, scrolling on a phone or watching old episodes of your favorite show. It's more active than looking at a screen, and it can open your mind to new places and ideas you've never dreamed of.

Want to get in the habit of reading? Create an inviting, cozy little reading corner in your house (even just a soft pillow or a blanket will do it). Don't force yourself to read books you think you "should" be reading. It's fine if you don't finish one and want to move on to the next. If mysteries aren't your thing, try sci-fi. Poems and short stories count too! Reading is best when you're truly into it, so try to get recommendations from people who know you well. There's no sweeter feeling than getting really absorbed in the world of a book only to look up and find that it's hours later!

Memorize

You're asked to memorize things all the time for school, but there are other ways to test our memories. Play with memory cards, sudoku, or word-train games. (We love the classic "I'm Going on Vacation," where each person repeats everyone else's packing items before adding one of their own.) Learn every word of your new favorite song by listening to small bits of it over and over, so you can impress your friends at the next birthday party. Music is a great way to memorize things for school: next time you have a geography quiz, try singing the answers in the tune of a song. Rhymes also help, so why not write a poem?

Our bodies can memorize moves too. Learn a new dance in front of the mirror. Study a basketball trick on YouTube and try it, then try again (and again). Eventually your arms and legs will do the next step without you having to think so hard. When it comes to memorization, repetition and patience are key.

Focus and Breathe

There are times when the world will throw lots of things at you all at once. Birthday parties, but also homework, but also family time, but also swim practice . . . it's a lot! Or maybe nothing will be happening—you'll be in bed, with the light off, trying to sleep—but your mind will be buzzing with all the thoughts of the day. Or maybe you have a big science project to do on a winter night, but you can't focus because your mind keeps drifting to thoughts of sunny days or that time you splashed in a creek and caught crayfish.

During these moments, it really helps to just be still. And breathe. Try slowly filling your belly with air . . . in for four counts . . . hold for four counts . . . out for four counts. If you come across a stressful thought, wave to it but then say goodbye to it. If you're having trouble focusing on one thing, pick a color and look around the room, finding all the shades of that same color. You can also turn on your five senses and make a mental list of things around you: one thing in the room that you can see, one you can feel, one you can taste, one you can hear, and one you can smell.

These simple exercises will quiet all those racing thoughts and tell your brain to come back to the present. You'll feel the calm come back to your body, and things will start to feel less overwhelming. Adults call this "mindfulness," but you can come up with any code words you want, like "quiet time."

Let It Go

Ambition and hard work are both great things . . . in moderation. Sometimes, though, we put too much pressure on ourselves to get everything right 100 percent of the time. Not one human on this Earth can be perfect all the time. So this desire—also known as **perfectionism**—will always make us sad and frustrated eventually.

It sounds great to always say the right thing, or know all the answers, or have a great hair day every day. Alas, that's just not possible. Plus, making mistakes and generally being our awesomely imperfect selves are how we learn and grow.

In our busy world, there are lots of ways to seek validation from others. When you get a good grade or look cute on social media, people in your life shower you with all kinds of rewards and approval, and that feels good. Of course it does! But chasing that feeling is where you run into trouble, because if you try and fail to be perfect (you will), you may lose confidence and blame yourself.

It's fine—it's great!—to care about doing a good job and challenge yourself to be better. It's also natural to juggle school and sports and art and friendship. We all want lives that are full, interesting, and exciting. But you need to be able to do those things for yourself and not to please others.

Here's one thing you need to remember: sometimes it's okay to simply Let. Things. Go. Did you miss a few questions on that geography quiz? Is your hair having an off day? It's really, truly not the end of the world. This is where those breathing skills can come in handy. In for four . . . hold for four . . . out for four . . . it's going to be okay. In calm moments, remind yourself: stumbling can be good. It can teach you what *not* to do in the future.

Don't waste your mistakes. By wallowing or worrying constantly about a mistake, you're preventing yourself from thinking about all the things you learned from the mistake. Being a Rebel Girl isn't about getting everything perfect. It's about having courage and taking risks, and how will you do that if you're terrified to fail?

Are You a Perfectionist?

1. What does your bedroom look like right now?

A. Clean and tidy. Everything is in its place.
B. I forgot to make my bed, but other than that, it's neat!
C. There are some clothes on the floor and papers scattered on my desk—cleaning day is tomorrow.
D. It looks pretty messy, but I know where everything is—I promise!

2. How do group projects make you feel?

A. Annoyed, because I usually have to do everything myself
B. A little uneasy, but as long as tasks are assigned, it'll work out
C. Good! I love collaborating on ideas.
D. Group projects are my favorite, especially when I'm in a group with my friends.

3. What do you like better, baking or cooking?

A. Baking! I like following a recipe exactly.
B. Baking, because I like to decorate cakes and cupcakes at the end
C. Cooking, because you can make it up as you go along
D. Neither, but I like trying new foods

4. When you make a mistake, what do you tell yourself?

A. *How could I be so dumb? I can't believe I did that!*
B. *That was silly of me, but I'll do better next time.*
C. *Things happen, but it's not the end of the world.*
D. *Welp, guess I won't do that again. Moving on!*

5. **You got a bad grade on a spelling test even though you studied. What's your next step?**

   A. Cancel all my plans so I can study even harder for the next one
   B. Schedule some time after school with my teacher to understand what I did wrong
   C. Switch study tactics and see if that works better
   D. Just accept that spelling isn't my thing

6. **After a long week, how do you like to relax on Friday evening?**

   A. By practicing the piano for my recital
   B. Go for a brisk bike ride around my neighborhood
   C. Pizza and a movie with my family
   D. A sleepover with all my friends!

7. **You're running short on time while working on a craft project. What do you do?**

   A. Finish up what I can and save the rest for later. I want to give it my full attention.
   B. I'd pick up my pace but still try to keep everything as neat as I can.
   C. Rush to finish it. It's okay if it's a little messy—it's not going in a museum.
   D. Skip over some details. I just want to get it done.

Answers

MOSTLY As: PRETTY MUCH A PERFECTIONIST

You really like things to be organized, and you're always striving to be the best you can be. These are admirable qualities, but remember to cut yourself some slack! No one is perfect, no matter how hard they try, and messing up is how we learn and grow.

MOSTLY Bs: QUITE BALANCED

You're driven to succeed, but you know that it's not healthy to put too much pressure on yourself. If things don't go according to your plan, that's okay. It might be tough to feel this balanced all the time, but it's a good goal to strive for!

MOSTLY Cs: MOSTLY CAREFREE

You're a big-picture person. You don't let little things get you down, and you move on from mistakes quickly. Well done, you! Certain things—like writing essays—do require attention to detail, though, so pay close attention when you're working through those types of things.

MOSTLY Ds: TOTALLY RELAXED

You're rarely stressed or worried and like to take things as they come instead of overthinking them. Awesome! It's great to feel calm, but be sure to carve out some time for introspection here and there. Thinking through what we can be better at helps us become smarter and stronger.

GOOD RISKS AND BAD RISKS: HOW TO TELL THE DIFFERENCE

This is going to get a little confusing. We're supposed to take risks, but we're also supposed to make smart decisions.

How do we know which risks are worth it and which aren't?

Honestly, even adults struggle with this question. That's the whole trouble with risk: it means being okay with the unknown. If we never take risks, we'll stay in the same familiar, sometimes boring place we've always been. Taking a risk can be a brave, admirable, empowering thing to do. But if we always choose the riskier option, we open ourselves to discomfort, frustration, and even danger. (And we might also let people down or hurt their feelings.)

How do you find a balance between these two sides?

As we know, the part of the brain that's in charge of good decisions is still developing at your age. So the first step is to understand that you might not always make the right choice. But the more you practice being thoughtful and taking a pause before you do things, the better you'll get at choosing the right path.

Let's ponder some examples. Which decisions seem like risks worth taking? What sounds too risky?

Ruby's friend scores some tickets to see a band she loves. No, seriously, this is Ruby's absolute favorite band. She's dying to go to her first concert. The only problem is, it's three hours away, and her friend's sister is leaving in her car right after school. Going to the concert would mean skipping volleyball practice just before championships and definitely not studying for a math quiz she has the next day. Ruby is the team captain, so her teammates are relying on her. On the other hand, it's a rare opportunity for Ruby to listen live to the songs she loves. Should she go?

Kaya hears through the grapevine that a group of parents are trying to remove some of her favorite books from her school's library. Toni Morrison's *The Bluest Eye*, Ashley Hope Pérez's *Out of Darkness*, and even *The Diary of Anne Frank* might get yanked off the shelf. This feels wrong to her. Some students are planning to protest outside a PTA meeting on Thursday night, even though the principal has warned that it might lead to suspension. Should Kaya show up?

Sofia was at a sleepover last weekend when one of her friends did something that really hurt her feelings: she made fun of Sofia for sleeping with her mouth open, and everyone laughed. Sofia thought about it all week. She kept reliving how mortified and small she felt. Back at school, the girls at the sleepover are still ribbing Sofia about it—and it's bothering her. Should she rock the boat and confront her friend about how she feels?

All of the risks involved in these scenarios have consequences, and they also all have rewards. None of them has an easy answer. So, when in doubt . . .

Go with Your Gut

Sometimes the best way to make a judgment call is to listen to your gut. Not literally—the stomach rumbles you hear are probably hunger pangs, not intuition. Still, our bodies do often give us signs when we're faced with a tough decision, and it can be a way to distinguish right from wrong. Ruby might want to impulsively follow her desire to go see her favorite band, for instance, but then she feels it: a nagging sensation, a chill throughout her body. Her heart says *Yes! Go!* but a few more minutes of thinking might make her realize that she'd be letting down her volleyball teammates and putting her math grade at risk.

Sometimes, negative consequences are worth the risk. Getting suspended from school is a big deal, for example, but standing up for what you believe in is also important. The banned books situation might be one that Kaya talks over with trusted friends, parents, or teachers before making a decision (also known as a "gut check"). Deciding whether to take a risk doesn't have to be a lonely process!

And then, there are the no-brainers—you'll know these when you see them. Sofia telling her friend about her hurt feelings after the sleepover might be terrifying, especially since that friend has a little bit of a temper. Sofia may worry that she won't want to be her friend anymore, or that she'll tell everyone Sofia's a crybaby. But with a little confidence and courage, Sofia knows she'll feel better in the long run that she stood up for herself. And if the worst happens anyway? She'll know that this person isn't kind or understanding enough to be her true friend.

Your emotions are running wild right now, and you are going to be very tempted to make decisions based on what you urgently want in that instant. (Who doesn't want to trade responsibility for fun?) But you are also growing up, and that means remembering the wisdom you've picked up from parents, friends, and past experiences. Often you know the right answer for you, deep down. Just take a moment to consider how you'll feel about it in the future.

Sometimes After We Take Risks . . . We Fail

Okay, so you've listened to your gut, taken the risk, and then . . . something goes terribly wrong. Don't panic! That doesn't mean the risk wasn't worth taking. It just means you're feeling pretty low right now. (Not forever, just right now.) Let's take a look at another situation.

Picture This:

Maya had stage fright, but she'd also always dreamed of being in musicals. Costumes, makeup, stage lights . . . she loved it all. Maya gathered up the courage to audition for *Matilda*—she thought she'd make a great Miss Trunchbull. She memorized the song "The Hammer" and practiced with her mom dozens of times. She really thought she'd nail it. But on the audition day, her fear got the best of her, and she totally blanked. Like, could not remember the very first line when the music started. She stumbled through the whole thing, singing off-tune and turning beet-red in front of every other student auditioning. Not only had she probably blown her chance to be in the musical, but also everyone witnessed her mistake. She was mortified.

Maya experienced her worst fear: a terrible, public embarrassment. And yet! Mistakes and failure didn't kill Maya—and they won't kill you either! An epic fail doesn't erase the incredible bravery you have inside of you to take a risk, even if it goes awry. As Taylor Swift said in her commencement speech at NYU: "Learn to live alongside cringe."

Foolproof Guide to Moving On After an Epic Fail

Be your own reassuring bestie. This is a perfect moment to be kind to yourself, not beat yourself up. How do you do that? Simple: just picture what you would say to your best friend if she were going through the same thing. You'd remind her of all her good qualities, right? You'd rub her back and say you admired her for putting herself out there, even if it didn't turn out like she pictured. Then you'd make a dumb joke and try to entice her with something fun. Speaking of . . .

Go do something you love. Don't wallow in the same space as the mistake—change the scenery, immediately. Grab a friend and visit your favorite pizza spot or bookstore or museum. Watch a movie that will make you laugh. The goal is distraction. Obsession never made anyone feel better. But a scoop of your favorite ice cream? It's practically guaranteed to cheer you up.

Get some perspective. It can be really hard to picture the future, so try instead to remember your past. When was the last time you failed at something you tried or embarrassed yourself in front of a lot of people? Maybe it was when you were in a hurry to get to class, tripped, and landed on your butt. Ouch—not a great memory. But be honest: does anyone still talk about it or even remember it? Do *you* even think about it anymore? Maybe you're even laughing about it now. Luckily, that's exactly what's going to happen to this latest fail. It will shock you how much it fades into the background or becomes a good story you and your friends can appreciate.

Keep trying! Just because something you try doesn't go as planned doesn't mean you shouldn't stop trying. It just means you have to keep being brave and going for what you want. In the immortal words of the singer Aaliyah: "Dust yourself off and try again." Now that you've survived the worst-case scenario, you can stop being afraid of it.

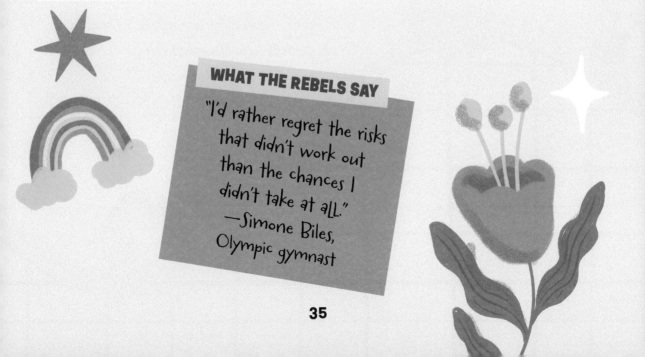

WHAT THE REBELS SAY

"I'd rather regret the risks that didn't work out than the chances I didn't take at all."
—Simone Biles, Olympic gymnast

THE FEELINGS ROLLER COASTER

One day, all of a sudden, your moods may feel completely out of your control. You might randomly swing from one mood-vine to the next. A tiny tiff with your sibling can flood your body with rage. One glance from your crush can ruin any chance of finishing your homework. A friend's slightly mean comment can feel like the actual end of the world. And when you feel happiness, you really feel it. When everyone is laughing at your jokes at the pool party, and it's a beautiful day, and there's delicious post-swimming snacks, you're in heaven and you never want that feeling to end.

There's nothing wrong with you! Hormones, the chemicals in your body that cause puberty and body changes, are also causing your emotions to run wild. These moods often feel like a room without a window: it's impossible to see your way out of them. You might be thinking: *I guess this is how I'm going feel for the rest of my life.* Not quite.

Even when you're deep in a windowless mood, there are ways to come back to reality and remind yourself how strong, smart, funny, and capable you are. From the big joys to the dark lows, the best way to get through these big moods is to deeply experience them . . . and then let them go.

Powerful moods are normal, but they don't have to overpower you.

First things first: give yourself a break! What's going on inside your body is truly wild, an experience unlike anything it has gone through before. Remember: your brain is busy prepping for adulthood's complex and potent emotions—it just hasn't learned how to regulate them yet. You may have grown-ups in your life who seem amused by your strong moods, like they're no big deal. We are here to tell you that your feelings are real, they're valid, and they're nothing to be ashamed of.

As we walk through many of the emotions you'll be experiencing, you'll see that you have the power to stay positive and focused even aboard the "feelings roller coaster."

SO MANY EMOTIONS

The sheer number of distinct feelings your brain is capable of can seem endless! Sometimes we'll feel a dozen of them in one day. Other times we'll have a stretch of cheeriness that makes us feel light as air. Here are just a few of the emotions you might encounter more and more as you grow up.

Envy and Jealousy

It's tough to think of more unpleasant emotions than jealousy and envy. They're slightly different things: they both mean that you desire something another person has, but jealousy has an air of hostility and competitiveness, while envy might feel more like admiration. No matter how it shows up, these feelings are truly the worst! And, unfortunately, common.

The best way to combat jealousy or envy is to attack it at the root. Really think about why you're so jealous or envious of someone—is it because they are intentionally hurting you, or because of your own insecurities and fears? A lot of the time, it's the latter. That might be a bit . . . uncomfortable to think about. But rest assured, these emotions are normal. They're just not exactly rational. This is why it's perfectly okay to *feel* envy and jealousy, but it's almost never okay to act on them. Take out that journal, vent to a friend, cry into a pillow, but try hard not to lash out at the object of your jealousy.

Frustration

Frustration lies somewhere between anger and annoyance, and it can appear when there's nothing you can do to change a situation. It can show up when, say, your parents enforce rules you don't agree with, or when it rains on the day you plan a birthday party in the park. You may want to scream or kick the walls. Like anger, it's best to channel frustration away from the humans in your life. If you want to talk about your feelings with your sibling or grown-up, that's great! But if you feel like you are going to lash out because you're feeling crummy, it's best to direct the energy elsewhere. Take a run, do your breathing exercises, yell along to loud music. The release will make you feel instantly better.

Sometimes frustration happens when you don't understand something, like how to start your essay for science class, or how to advance to the next level in a video game. Everyone feels this way sometimes. Wanting to achieve a goal that is just beyond your grasp is no fun. It doesn't usually help to sink into that feeling or let it spiral into anger. But how do you break out of a frustration spiral? Take a break from whatever you're doing and go back to it when you're feeling fresh. You can also ask for some help figuring out whatever is puzzling you!

Guilt

Guilt isn't easy to describe, but we've all felt it: a kind of sinking feeling that might come when you feel you've let someone down, gone against your family or culture's beliefs, or violated your own values. It's an interesting emotion, because it can be hard to know whether you should be feeling guilty. Some guilt is good. It's telling you that you didn't act as well as you want to and that you feel bad about hurting someone else.

Pro tip: Sincere, heartfelt apologies, without excuses tacked onto them, work wonders!

Same with coming clean if you've lied or not given someone the whole truth. Not only is apologizing the right thing to do, but saying you're sorry (and what you're sorry for) and really meaning it also relieves guilt. Win-win all around!

Guilt is a problem only when it's excessive or goes on too long. If you've made amends, admitted you were wrong, or tried as hard as you could to fix a situation—that means you did your best. So forgive yourself! And if you feel guilt because you broke the taboos of your family or heritage, take some extra time to think about what *you* believe. As you get older, the values you hold dear might change from the ones you grew up with, and that's okay. As long as you're living according to your own moral code and doing your best to be kind to others and yourself, there's no need to feel guilty.

Confusion

Sometimes a grown-up will tell you to do something and you won't know where to start. Maybe your dad will ask you to mow the lawn, for example, but no one ever taught you how to use the lawnmower. Don't be afraid to ask for more information! It's healthy and helpful to ask for help or clarification when you aren't sure how to do something or if a situation is confusing.

Other times, it won't be so simple. Your brain will try to reach for an emotion or a decision, but it won't know quite which one to pick. Imagine this: your friend Alice tells you a secret about your other friend, Karla, and you're not sure if you should tell Karla what's going on. When you have mixed feelings about something, it is called **ambivalence**. A close cousin of confusion, ambivalence  can pull you in different directions (and sometimes leave you frozen in place). Advice might help a little, but ultimately it's *you* who figures your way out of this type of confusion. Weigh the pros and cons, sleep on it, and then go with your intuition.

Pride

Remember to celebrate the wins! Sometimes we get strong messages not to be openly proud of ourselves, even when we accomplish something major. We're told that we'll look like we're bragging or showing off. Not true! It's important to recognize when your hard work has paid off and to take a second to feel satisfied. Try standing in front of a mirror and congratulating yourself when you've done something you are proud of. Or speak up at dinner and tell your family about your exciting news. You did it, and you deserve to feel good about it.

Joy

As your world expands more and more, you'll find new ways to feel joy, excitement, and comfort. Whether it's a tattered blanket that's been soothing you since childhood or your newly discovered knack for ice-skating, keep all the things that make you happy at the front of your mind. These thoughts will come in handy when you're feeling down. (See page 59 for the "pick-me-up kit.") Try to do more of the things that bring you joy. If you love the feeling of getting lost in a good book, cuddle up with a great read every night. If playing baseball makes you smile, get outside with the neighborhood kids and hit your heart out. Hard work is important, and it might feel thankless if you don't have those joyful moments in between.

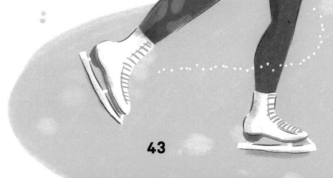

Bravery

Being brave is a fabulous quality to have—but it means different things depending on who you are. Trying out a new skill and venturing outside of your comfort zone are ways of being brave. It *can* mean facing your fear of heights and going on the highest roller coaster at the theme park, but it's also brave to speak up and say that you don't want to. Bravery requires confidence in yourself and your decisions. Speaking of . . .

Confidence

Simply put, having confidence is believing in oneself. It's one of the most important qualities to nurture as you grow up. Lots of things can challenge your confidence, from the star player on your basketball team to the girl in your class with the impossibly gorgeous curls. It doesn't help that the media often pokes holes in our confidence, whispering in our ear that we should do this, buy those, look like that.

It's important to guard your confidence like it's a rare, precious jewel.

WHAT THE REBELS SAY

"When I first tried roller-skating, I was scared, but I learned that I could do something even if I was scared or worried."
—Simone T., 10, California, USA

44

Confidence-Boosting 101

There are lots of ways to boost your confidence. Here are a few to try:

Master a skill, like a new gymnastics move. Working hard at something and achieving your goal will have you feeling like the star you are.

Find something you love and do more of it. Maybe you've discovered that you enjoy drawing, or writing, or training your dog to do new tricks. Whatever it is, focus on those things that bring you joy, and you'll feel your confidence soar!

Challenge yourself, even in small ways. If you'd like to make a few new friends, try talking to one new person each week at lunch. If you're itching to learn something new, offer to help cook dinner a few nights a week.

Celebrate how awesome you are. Always remember to look in the mirror and be your own biggest fan.

Anger

Your temper may feel more intense lately. Feelings of anger may spring up more easily and suddenly. You may feel yourself wanting to physically or emotionally hurt someone else. Or you might direct your rage inward, thinking ugly and unforgiving thoughts about yourself.

It's completely fine to express that anger, as long as it's not directed at a person—and that includes you! When you feel your anger well up, leave the scene. Scream or punch a pillow. Take a walk, run, or do another form of exercise. Rather than letting your anger spill everywhere, pour it into a safe place where it can't cause harm. Grab a pen and write down what's making you furious, using as many exclamation points as you want!!! Put on headphones and listen to angsty music—that's literally what it was invented for. Take a crack at making music or any other kind of art. And when your mood lifts (it will—we promise!), allow yourself to feel a little pride that you overcame those big feelings.

Picture This:

Dorie tried to be a model daughter all week. She fed the cat every morning, took out the trash without being asked, and got a perfect score on her science quiz. She was sure her parents were going to let her go to a sleepover at a new friend's house. But when she asked her mom about the weekend, she got a strong *no*. Dorie had to go to her great-aunt's funeral, and that was final.

"Family comes before sleepovers," her mom said. "Those are the rules." Dorie was beside herself with anger. "This is so unfair!" she wanted to yell. She barely knew this aunt, and this was a rare opportunity to get closer to a new friend she really liked. She felt her face getting hot. Her fists clenched into tight balls.

But instead of exploding in her mother's face, she went upstairs to her room to let it out in private. She furiously scribbled her thoughts in her diary. She turned up Olivia Rodrigo's "brutal" until she couldn't even hear her own thoughts. A few minutes later, she was calm enough to go back downstairs. Venting privately meant that she could accept her mom's decision, even though it made her upset. Progress!

STRESS, WORRY, AND ANXIETY, OH MY!

Nowadays, you're becoming more independent than ever, and your social life is getting more fun. The world is starting to treat you more like an adult, and that's exciting! But it can also be a whole lot, all at once. It might feel like you're buried under a big pile of competing responsibilities, and you can barely breathe under the heap.

It can be tough to ease feelings of stress and overwhelm. The "quiet time" we talked about—breathe in for four counts, hold for four counts, breathe out for four counts—can really help when it all feels like too much. Once you are feeling calm, you might want to take some time to unpack your feelings and see if you can pinpoint what is really stressing you out.

Picture This:

Carly went to the same elementary school as the other kids in the neighborhood, but then she scored big on a test for a private, STEM-focused middle school. Suddenly, the pressure was on. Schoolwork seemed galaxies harder than it used to. Gymnastics practice went from twice a week to four times a week. It seemed like all her friends at her new school knew how to play an instrument, and she felt like she had to, as well. So she signed up for piano lessons on top of everything else.

The pressure built and built, and pretty soon Carly felt overwhelmed. She was coming home late from her activities, then doing homework until bedtime. She didn't have time for friends or even to watch her favorite Netflix show. One day, it all came to a head, and she burst into tears. She was breathing fast, and her chest felt tight.

So she took a pause. She breathed in slowly, letting her belly get big with air, then blew it out in a satisfying gust. With her big sister's help, she sat down at her desk and made a list of everything she had going on in her life, drawing a heart next to activities she enjoyed and a frowny face next to activities that made her feel panicky. She realized that she didn't want to take gymnastics anymore, that it was eating up too much of her time. Later that night during dinner, Carly calmly announced to her parents that she'd thought about it a lot, and she wanted to quit the team. Impressed by her composure, they agreed. Phew!

How to Fight Against Worry

Reality is your friend during bouts of worry. It's important to be able to tell yourself that it's not as bad as it seems, even if you don't totally believe it. If you stress about one particular thing a lot, create a little safety net for the bad times: write down a string of rational, logical statements you can turn to when you've lost your grip on what's true and what isn't.

Helpful Phrases for Your Safety Net

* I have a few friends who love me no matter what.

* Everyone's insecure about something, even popular people. (They might even have more insecurity!)

* Popularity is a useless thing to chase.

* Most people are too worried with their own problems to be thinking so much about me.

* Even if people want to be mean about this latest drama, they'll move on pretty soon.

* I know I'm a kind, sensitive, powerful person.

* It's going to be okay!

Let's go through an example. Let's say you have this big worry: you had a misunderstanding with one of the most popular girls in your class, and now the whole school is mad at you. You can pull from the safety net list on the previous page to remind yourself of what's actually true, like that you have a few friends who love you no matter what or that popularity is a useless thing to chase. You can do this same exercise on the spot, if you find yourself with a cluster of worries all at the same time. Write down each worry in your journal and underneath respond to the worry in a logical way. Like this:

Big worry: I worry that I'm not going to make the travel soccer team.

Rational, logical statement: I've been practicing a lot, and I'm going to do my best and have fun. If I don't make it this season, I'll ask what I should work on and try again next time.

That Special Form of Stress: School!

Sabrina freaks out every time she has a big test at school. It's not only about the information on the actual test—she starts seeing the test as part of one long chain, stretching past high school and college and her first job and the rest of her life. *If I fail, it'll affect my whole future*, she thinks. *I'll never get into a good college, and I'll never get a good job, and I'll be a huge failure!*

Sabrina has something called **academic anxiety**. Once she started middle school, homework and tests really ramped up. People kept talking to her about high school and even college. So she started thinking about her education as something that can majorly affect her life. Pretty soon, she realized that school was becoming a source of stress.

Maybe you have similar thoughts like these—or maybe you don't! Either way, it's good to care about your schoolwork, and a sprinkling of nerves can keep you engaged and on your toes. But if it's feeling like it's too much, there are lots of things you can do to ease the jitters.

Create a Vibe

It's good to push away distractions, but you don't always have to lock yourself in a room hunched over a desk to study. If it's a beautiful day, find a private place in a park or your backyard and set up your books and flash cards on a blanket. If you must be in a room, use warm lighting. Research shows that fluorescent light can make anxiety worse. Make a playlist of wordless music to listen to. Instrumental music like classical and jazz is proven to help our brains focus.

Make Studying Fun

Draw pictures or comics to help your brain visualize scenarios for a history test. Make flash cards and decorate them with cheerful, bright colors. (There are also apps that create flash cards, if that's more your speed.) Create a bingo board with vocabulary words, write down the definitions, pull them out of a hat, and see if you can match them with their words. Puns, rhymes, or other forms of wordplay might also help you remember the info on a test. Come up with your own board game or role-play—it might take you a little longer than if you crammed with notebooks only, but the extra boost of fun just might be worth it.

Recruit Some Buddies (and Choose Them Wisely)

Studying with other people can make the time fly by, but it's a delicate balance: there are some friends who are going to be a little *too* fun to hang out with. Your best bet is to choose a friend you know only from class who also happens to enjoy the subject. You'll know they'll be serious about studying—but you can also take little breaks and get to know each other better.

Put It in Perspective

Keep in mind that even if the absolute worst thing happens and you bomb a test, your life is not over. It will not—we repeat, *not*—ruin your chances of succeeding. There's always the option of extra credit or just studying harder next time. Perfect grades are also not essential to doing well in college or a career down the road. Some of the smartest, most ambitious people weren't great students. Fact: Thomas Edison, one of the most famous inventors ever, was terrible at math. What we're saying is, everyone learns differently. Some people will never be awesome test-takers, and that's okay!

Take Care of Your Body

Staying up late studying might give you bragging rights, but we have some bad news for you: it's not going to set you up for success. The night before a test, try to go to sleep at your normal bedtime. Then eat a big, delicious breakfast the next day. Put aside five minutes to stretch your body, listen to a short meditation, or take some deep breaths. If your body feels relaxed, your mind will too!

What Is Anxiety, Exactly?

Anixety is like worrying, but more intense. It usually happens when you're unsure about the outcome of something, like a test, a trip, or a social interaction.

A little spike of anxiety right before a big event won't hurt you and can even be useful. You want to do well on that test tomorrow, which means you care about school . . . and that's good! Worries and fears can also help keep you safe. Remember that "fight-or-flight" response we discussed earlier? When you're in genuine danger, it can send signals to your body and flood it with certain hormones, like cortisol and adrenaline. Your stomach might hurt, you might get chills, or your heart might start beating fast. It could be your brain saying, "That hill isn't safe to ride your bike down!" Or it could be something feelings-related, like "This person makes me feel nervous and insecure. Maybe I don't actually want to be friends with them."

Anxiety becomes a problem only when it's excessive and feels out of your control. This might be what's called an **anxiety disorder**. When you have an anxiety disorder, it can feel similar to garden-variety stress, but you may feel it even when you aren't in an obviously stressful situation. An anxiety disorder might also affect your ability to determine fact from feeling. To an anxious person, an extreme fear (like their plane is going to crash) may start to just seem like a certain reality.

Some people who have extreme anxiety—or even people who don't—might experience **panic attacks**. They are not fun at all. Panic attacks send that fight-or-flight response into overdrive. A person having a panic attack might feel out of breath, dizzy, sweaty, or shaky. Their thoughts may speed up too. They might become afraid that there's something physically wrong with them.

Here's the good news: panic attacks can be managed. If the person experiencing them can recognize them for what they are, they can try to breathe through them and remind themself they're safe and that these feelings are only temporary. If they keep happening, help from a doctor or therapist might be necessary.

NAVIGATING THE BLUES

One of the hormones that spikes in your body during puberty is **estrogen**. This is mostly a good thing. It helps with the development of your breasts, hips, and body hair and the regulation of your period. The downside? It can also make you feel sad and sensitive during an already overwhelming time. This is very common, but sadness sure doesn't feel good when it's happening.

Like anger, sadness fades more easily when it has someplace to go. It's okay to lock yourself in your bedroom and really sink into your feelings, perhaps with a tearjerker book or a sappy song. And like anger, sadness can also inspire art, so pick up that pen, paintbrush, or musical instrument when you're feeling down. Decorate a journal and keep it close for any stray thoughts. Connect with your sweetest, most sympathetic friend who won't mind seeing or hearing you cry.

Gather objects, photos, snacks, and scents that lift your spirits so you'll have them ready next time you're feeling weepy.

Then, when you find yourself in a better mood, create ways to comfort a sadder you in the future. Hype yourself up: make a list of your most fantastic and unique qualities, think of 10 things in your life to be thankful for, then read it all when you're at a low point. Add these lists to a "pick-me-up kit."

Your pick-me-up kit could include:

* A photo strip from your best friend's birthday party
* A lotion with a scent you love
* A cool shell you found on the beach over the summer
* Colored pencils and a coloring book

When It's More Than Just a Downer Day

Not all sad feelings are easily soothed this way. If you're feeling extended periods of extreme misery and hopelessness, sleeping a lot, struggling to focus on school, or feeling like you want to harm yourself, tell an adult you trust as soon as possible. Those are signs of depression, not just run-of-the-mill sadness, and they require outside help from a therapist or doctor.

If one of these people thinks you have depression, take comfort in the fact that you are far from alone. It's very common. One out of five kids will have some form of depression before they reach adulthood, but only one-third of them are being treated for it. There's absolutely, positively *no shame* in getting some help. It'll make you feel better and teach you some new skills to handle your low moments.

Tips for Coping with Depression

Depression zaps you of energy, so it may feel like climbing Mount Everest to do even small things to feel better. We get it! Taking the first step is always the hardest.

Here's something surprising to know: behavior can change emotions. It may seem like the other way around—you're going home right after school instead of hanging with friends or doing activities because you're depressed—but actually, you might be feeling depressed because you're staying home. Changing your actions even a little bit can reorganize your thoughts and, finally, your feelings.

There are a few strategies you can try on your own when you find yourself wallowing too long, or if your sadness is really getting in the way of a happy life. And if they're not enough? Consider therapy. Seriously, it can work wonders!

Reach Out

It may feel embarrassing to admit you're sad. You might also feel guilty for not being as fun as you used to be. But talking to just *one* person about how you feel can be a game changer. It'll make you feel less alone and maybe even help you figure out ways to feel better. If you don't feel like getting into all that, even keeping it light during lunch with a friend might boost your mood. Seeing someone's face in person is better than texting (but it's also okay to text if that's all you can do right now).

Pet Your Dog
(or Cat, or Guinea Pig)

Animals are great because they don't judge, they're great listeners, and they keep you company. Take a few minutes to cuddle your dog or make your cat purr. (Or a friend's dog or cat, if you don't have pets.) Caring for a sweet little animal, who is always in a good mood, can help get you out of your head for a moment.

Go Outside

Taking a walk and getting some sunshine on your face can be a welcome change of pace when you're feeling down. Plus, moving your body activates chemicals designed to make you feel good. A fast walk (or even a run) can get those chemicals flowing even faster. Time outside is good for your physical health too. Getting fresh air will help you sleep better at night, which can do wonders to improve your mood. Also, seeing people out and about, even if they're strangers, can remind you that there's a big, exciting world out there.

WHAT THE REBELS SAY

"I saw an opportunity to . . . normalize conversations around mental health and just say: 'It's okay to be sad. It's okay to not always feel good.' Everyone has bad days."
—Te Manaia Jennings, painter and mental-health advocate

How to Help a Friend Who's Feeling Down

We talked about connection being one of the most important steps for combating depression—but it's also really hard to do when you're stuck in your own sadness. If you see a friend struggling, make it easier for them. Go ahead and reach out, even if they haven't been reaching out to you. Ask gentle, open-ended questions like, "Been thinking about you. How are you?" The best thing you can do right now is listen. Make them feel heard but try not to give advice. Even saying something like, "That sounds so hard. I'm sorry," can be comforting for someone going through it. They also might not feel like talking, and that's okay too. All you have to do is let them know you're there for them if they need you—whenever they need you.

If your friend seems really, *really* depressed, don't be afraid to tap a trusted adult on the shoulder. Your first instinct may be to drop everything and support them, but you should never take on that burden alone. Talk to an understanding parent or a school counselor. That's what they're there for.

LOSS OF A LOVED ONE

There is a special word for the pain of losing a family member or someone close to you: **grief**. The word kind of sounds exactly how it feels—rough and painful. It often feels bigger and more intense than sadness. Even though death is part of life and everyone will be touched by it, the pain of someone not being there for you in the same way they used to be is still heartbreaking. The good news is, there are steps you can take to honor your feelings when someone dies and keep the memory of that person close to you.

Grieve the way you need to. When some people hear about the death of a friend, family member, or pet, they cry right away. Others may not shed a tear for days, weeks, or months—or ever. Some people want to be alone to remember their loved one. Others may want to talk about what happened. There are lots of different ways of handling a death, and there is no right way or wrong way.

Make time to remember.
After someone dies, you may go to a funeral or memorial service. This is a time to celebrate the person's life and grieve with family and friends. People might tell

stories about the person or read their favorite poem. If you were close to the person who died, people might come up to you and say things like "I'm so sorry for your loss." You can reply with "thank you" or "thank you for coming." If it feels too public to express your feelings at a big gathering, you and your grown-up can take some time alone together to look at pictures and talk about the person who died. Either way, dedicating some time to remembering them will help with your grieving process.

Talk about it. As time goes on, your sadness will become less intense, but you still might suddenly miss the person who died, which can be a little jarring. You don't have to sit with these feelings alone. Talk to your grown-up or a friend when you're feeling sad. It can help to name these emotions and get them out in the open instead of letting them stew inside you.

Do a simple thoughtful action when others are grieving. If your best friend's grandmother just passed away, maybe you and your grown-up can make a lasagna and drop it off. That way, the grieving family doesn't have to think about making dinner for a couple of nights while they make funeral plans and process their sadness. You can also make a mental note to check in with your friend about how she's feeling in a few days or weeks. After someone dies, there's a lot of activity and attention just after it happens, but then people move on. That's a good time to let your friend know you're thinking of her.

THERAPY CAN HELP

So let's say you've tried lots of tactics to manage your anxiety, depression, or grief, and they're just not working. It might be time to find a therapist. Therapy comes in lots of different forms. You could end up seeing a social worker, a mental-health counselor, a psychologist, or a psychiatrist.

A therapist is a nonjudgmental, objective professional who is trained to help you with your worries and make life easier to manage. Therapists use many different theories and methods. Therapy might mean talking directly about what's bothering you, or it might mean playing games or drawing pictures. It might also mean breathing, meditating, or doing exercises to change your behavior. It might even mean taking medicine. There are special kinds of therapists who know how to help kids of color, LGBTQIA+ people, and kids who are having a rough time at home. It really depends on how old you are and what you're struggling with.

Therapy can help with all kinds of situations. Your reason might be an overall

feeling of depression. Or maybe you're struggling with a bully at school. Therapy can help if you're feeling confused or lost about your identity. It can also help if you're sure of your identity but your community isn't very accepting of it. The possibilities are endless. If you have a problem, trust us, there's a therapist out there who can help.

If you think you may need to see a therapist, don't stress! There's nothing wrong with seeking out a little help. In fact, you can pat yourself on the back for deciding to see a therapist. It's mature and empowering to decide to take care of yourself! Sometimes we get the idea that we could feel happier if we just try harder or have willpower to change. But mental-health issues are sometimes out of our control.

Mental-health issues are not that different from physical pain. When you have a sore throat or the flu, you don't handle it on your own, right? You and your grown-up head to the doctor. It's the same way with therapists—they step in when your brain and heart are hurting. Therapists are trained to understand the problems you're having and come up with a solution, whether that means medication, de-stressing strategies, or just talking it out.

Mindful Break

Scan the code to learn an exercise about facing your fears and anxieties.

Should I Go to Therapy?

How do you know if therapy will be helpful for you? Here are some questions to ask:

* Do you spend more than an hour a day feeling down or anxious?
* Are your worries, fears, or sadness making it hard to do schoolwork or activities that used to make you happy?
* Do you feel the need to hide how you feel from other people in your life?
* Is your sleep all wonky? Like, are you sleeping too much or having insomnia (not being able to sleep)?
* Are you feeling out of control of your emotions—not once in a while, but a lot of the time?
* Do you sometimes shrug your shoulders at the world and feel like you just don't care?

A yes to any of these means you might consider seeing a therapist. But how?

Finding a Therapist

One of the best things about therapy is that it's a safe time and place to discuss your most private thoughts with someone who will keep those thoughts private. But you do need an adult to help you find a therapist. Not everyone is comfy talking to their parents about their worries, but in most cases, you need their permission (and probably their health insurance) to start seeing a therapist. This is a time to be brave and open up to your grown-ups.

You can tell them a bit about what's bothering you and explain that you think talking to an unbiased person outside your everyday life might help. Try saying something like "I'm having a hard time lately. I'm feeling down a lot of the time. Will you help me find a therapist?" Once you've decided to try therapy, there's something important to keep in mind: therapy is a commitment. But doing the required homework—things like journaling and mindfulness exercises—can be super helpful for those who are struggling.

WHAT THE REBELS SAY

"I'm not embarrassed about any of the time I need to take to help myself, because that's making me a better me."
—Kristen Bell, actor and author

What to Expect from a First Therapy Appointment

It's the night before your first therapy appointment, and you're nervous. We get it! It might ease your mind if you know what to expect. Here are a few things to keep in mind:

You don't have to prepare for the appointment. There's no need to "make a good impression" or be more "together" than you normally are. Just be yourself—even if that means you're sad or worried or tired. There's no such thing as failing at therapy.

You don't have to reveal more than you feel comfortable with. Come with an open mind, but it's also okay to offer facts about your life and your emotions at your own pace. This is your therapy. You can set the tone and the pace.

If you don't like your therapist, you can choose another one. Therapy can be expensive, even with insurance. So listen to your gut: if you're not feeling this therapist, shop around!

WHAT IF YOUR BRAIN JUST WORKS A LITTLE DIFFERENTLY?

One of the coolest things about people is that we're all different and so our minds all work a little differently too. This is called **neurodiversity**. It's a big word with a simple meaning: we're all unique in the way we learn, socialize, and process emotions. Conditions like autism, ADHD, or dyslexia are just some examples of the super interesting differences among human minds.

Autism is a condition that affects how someone's brain develops. Kids with autism tend to have trouble making friends, talking, dealing with a change in their routines, or staying calm around loud noises or bright lights. They might repeat words or move in a particular way. People often refer to the autism "spectrum," which means that some people have lots of these qualities, and others have fewer of them or they're less intense.

ADHD has a couple of different forms. There's "inattentive ADHD" (what people used to call ADD), which means that someone has trouble focusing or listening. People with inattentive ADHD are easily distracted and sometimes forgetful. Someone with hyperactive impulse ADHD has boundless energy, may fidget a lot, and can't seem to sit still. This condition is fairly common— more than 1 out of 10 kids are diagnosed with it.

Dyslexia is a learning disorder. When kids learn to read, the major puzzle piece that clicks into place is that speech sounds correspond to letters and words. People with dyslexia have trouble doing this decoding. This has nothing to do with their

intelligence. With extra attention and a learning programs tailored to their needs, kids with dyslexia are able to succeed and do well in school.

The idea behind neurodiversity is that there's no right way for a mind to process information, and that differences should be celebrated rather than "cured." People with these conditions call themselves **neurodivergent**, whereas people without these conditions are **neurotypical**. Neurodivergent people can often be very productive and lead full lives. They just need special considerations—the same way someone who's in a wheelchair needs a ramp. There are countless of examples of neurodivergent people who have accomplished incredible things. For instance, Temple Grandin, a professor of animal sciences, invented groundbreaking ways to improve the well-being of livestock on farms.

If some of the neurodivergent traits discussed here sound like you, talk to an adult and ask them if they can hook you up with a doctor who can do an evaluation. Try to resist the urge to google signs of ADHD or autism. You'll get flooded with information that might not necessarily help. Best to wait until you can talk to a professional—hopefully one who will treat you with respect and sensitivity.

WHAT THE REBELS SAY

"The world is going to need all of the different kinds of minds to work together."
—Temple Grandin, professor of animal sciences

How to Be a Good Friend to a Neurodivergent Person

Let's say you're neurotypical, but you just met someone with autism and you want to become closer friends. The key words here are **acceptance**, **patience**, and **empathy**. It's not always easy for neurotypical people to be friends with neurodivergent people. Neurodivergent people might not adhere to accepted social rules, and it might be jarring at first when they behave differently than what we typically consider polite or sociable. Just remember

that those social rules were set up for neurotypical people. Try to imagine what it's like to live in a world where tons of everyday expectations aren't tailored for your brain.

There may be some initial awkwardness to get past as you both learn about each other. But once you do, you may start to really appreciate each other's unique strengths and talents. Appreciating difference is a crucial skill in life!

Now that I've learned how brains work, I'll keep in mind (no pun intended) that each and every person's brain functions in its own special way. There are so many emotions to feel during our lifetime—all normal and just another example of how awesome the human brain really is. Even when chemicals in my brain are making me feel sad or angry, it's still pretty phenomenal to remember just how many different emotions and ideas it's capable of producing. Because without our thoughts and feelings, where would we be?

75

ASK THE EXPERTS

School is a lot of fun. You get to learn new things, discover what you're best at, and hang out with your friends. But there are some tricky things to navigate too. We sent some questions to Aline Topjian, a social emotional learning consultant, to get her take on handling school stress.

This year, I've been getting stressed out about how much homework I have. How do I manage my time?
—Caroline P., 13, Idaho, USA

It's completely normal to feel stressed and overwhelmed about homework. The good news is there are strategies and tools that can help you manage your time and reduce your stress.

First, find a place in your house where you can do your homework every day. Maybe that's your quiet bedroom, or maybe it's at the kitchen counter while your grown-up makes dinner. Whatever works for you! Similarly, try to stick to a consistent schedule. For example, you could say that every day after school, you'll come home, have a snack and take a 10-minute break, and then get started on your homework. Using tools like planners and to-do lists are also super helpful in terms of staying organized and on top of all your assignments. Arrange your assignments by deadlines. And once you finish an assignment, cross it off your list. This can help you feel accomplished! Lastly, take short breaks between assignments. Light physical activity, such as stretching or walking, can really help you regain focus.

First things first: your learning disability has nothing to do with how smart you are! Some of the brightest and most successful people in the world have learning disabilities. Another thing to keep in mind is that we all learn differently and have different strengths and weaknesses, regardless of whether we have a learning disability. Write down all the things you're amazing at and refer back to that list when you're feeling low.

Another important thing you can do is find help and support. For instance, if you struggle with reading comprehension, ask if you can meet with your teacher after school to go over the assigned reading and make sure you fully grasped it. Additionally, see if you can find other kids in your class or school who have similar learning disabilities. They'll probably be easy to find—up to 20 percent of Americans have one. This means 2 out of every 10 of your classmates probably have a learning disability. Finding a support group and knowing you're not alone will make things easier to manage.

Aline Topjian, social emotional learning consultant

Our readers and listeners had some great questions about mental health, so we reached out to psychotherapist Alexandra Vaccaro to answer them. Check out her tips for handling anxiety and keeping positive below.

I know everyone gets anxious, but what are ways people deal with it?
—Aubree F., 9, New York, USA

You are absolutely correct—everyone at some point experiences anxious feelings. There are a variety of coping skills that can help manage this sometimes difficult emotion. Mindfulness techniques are really great to learn because they help you calm your mind and body about the worries you are having and focus on the present moment. There is a breathing exercise in the chapter you just read, and you can take it a step further. It has a few names, but I call it box breathing. Box breathing is super simple. The first step is to draw a square on a piece of paper. Glide your finger up the side of the square while taking a deep breath in and counting to four. Then glide your finger across the top of the square as you hold that breath for another count of four. When you glide your finger down the other side of the square, exhale to the count of four. Then take a rest as you go along the bottom of the square before you start again. Do as many rounds as you need until you begin to feel the worry leave your body.

Our minds are very powerful and love to play tricks on us. Sometimes our minds make us believe we don't have control of our own thoughts and feelings. But guess what? We have complete control over how we feel simply with the thoughts we have. When we are able to have consistent positive thoughts of hope and happiness, even when some days just kind of stink, we will feel happier. One way to practice this is to keep a gratitude journal. Every day, write down three things you're grateful for. It can be big things like your family or small things like the delicious strawberry you ate that day. Challenges and bad days will come up, but when our minds are strong, we are better able to conquer life's curveballs.

**Alexandra Vaccaro,
Psychotherapist**

Let's Chat

Scan the code to listen to a conversation between our experts and girls just like you!

CHAPTER 2

My Body Is Strong

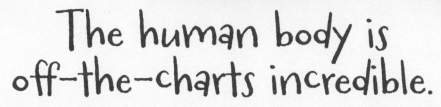

The human body is off-the-charts incredible.

It can climb mountains, give birth to babies, and hit home runs. Sure, I can't do all of those things now—and not everyone will be able to do that stuff (and that's okay!). But if the conditions were right, and I worked hard, maybe, just maybe, I could be a triathlete or belly dancer or astronaut or something I don't even know exists yet. Bodies come in all shapes and sizes, and they are changing all the time. Sometimes my body feels good and relaxed, and other times it causes me frustration and pain. Especially now— it's growing and changing in a way it never has before. Which can be a little scary, but it's also amazing. My body is good to me, and I love it.

82

YOUR BODY AND HOW IT WORKS, IN A NUTSHELL

Pretty soon, if it hasn't already, your body is going to morph and grow in new ways—which is exciting! But even way before you hit this phase, your body is a perfect system of many moving parts. We'll get to talking about boobs and body hair, but first let's explore the basics: a few ways your fantastic, capable body keeps you healthy and strong.

Your Strong Muscles

When the doctor says, "Make a muscle," you might think of flexing a bulgy bicep. But you have more than 600 muscles in your body, and some of them work without flexing anything at all. Muscles help you lift a suitcase or jump on a bed, but they also do things like keep your blood moving. They are made up of an elastic material with thousands upon thousands of fibers in each one.

The ones you can control and sometimes see—the ones that look like red stripes of licorice candy in the diagrams you see at school—are called **skeletal muscles**. These muscles are usually attached to bones thanks to things called **tendons**. When you flex a muscle to exercise or lift something, the tendons and bones come along with it. Some of the strongest, most visible muscles you have are in places like your thigh, calf, and upper arm. But there are also smaller ones doing constant work, like the muscles in your neck, hands, and even your face. Facial muscles work a little differently from skeletal muscles because they're sometimes attached to your skin rather than your bones. They're responsible for making you frown or smile or stick your tongue out at your little sister—all those millions of facial expressions we all make every single day. Muscles even help us talk. Your tongue is made up entirely of muscles—eight, to be exact.

Then there are muscles that work on their own without you having to think about them: the muscles that allow you to swallow, for example, or hold in (and push out) pee. These are called **smooth muscles**, and they're all over your body helping things run, well, smoothly.

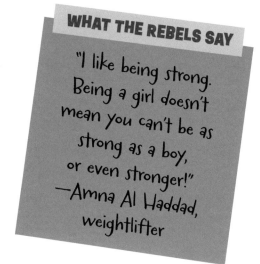

There's also that essential, involuntary group of muscles nestled in your chest called **cardiac muscles**. They make sure your heart pumps blood around your body. Ever wonder what exactly a heartbeat is? Yup, that's right, it's these muscles contracting, then relaxing.

The Bare-Bones of Bones

Many of our muscles simply wouldn't work without our 206 bones. Skeletal muscles stretch over our bones and joints to help us move and give our body power. They also protect our internal organs. You may be used to thinking of bones as dead (that creepy skeleton model in your biology class, for instance, or dinosaur bones at the museum). But the bones inside a body are as alive as they come—and, like the rest of you, they're constantly growing when you're a kid.

Bones are made up of a few different layers: the **periosteum**, **compact bone**, **cancellous bone**, and **bone marrow**. The periosteum is the outer layer of the bone, a crucial membrane that protects your bones, helps them grow, and repairs them if they break. Compact bone is what we all think of as simply "bone"—the hard, smooth, off-white layer. Under *that*, we have lots of layers of the cancellous bone, otherwise known as spongy bone (because it looks like, you guessed it, a sponge). These layers also support the bone, but they are more lightweight and flexible than compact bone. And in many bones, bone marrow lies inside all of these layers. Bone marrow has the consistency of jelly and makes all kinds of blood cells for our bodies.

Your thigh bone is your strongest bone. It can support up to *30 times* the weight of your body. That's a whole classroom of you-sized things! Pretty cool, huh? Other bones are delicate, like the 27 bones in your hand, all of which work together to help you throw a ball, type out texts, and grab handfuls of popcorn. Many bones are visible or touchable under your skin, like your skull and your spine and your collarbones.

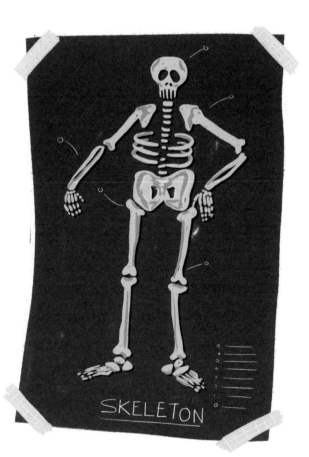

SKELETON

Even though bones' entire purpose is to protect your body and make you strong, they can also break . . . which means they need protection of their own. Don't forget to wear a helmet if you ride a bike, or protective gear if you play sports like soccer or hockey. And be sure to eat foods with calcium in them—like milk, cheese, yogurt, almonds, and leafy greens—to make sure your bones stay strong and grow nicely.

Your Own Personal Bodyguard: Your Immune System

Your immune system majorly has your back. It's made up of a whole network of organs, cells, and proteins, all trained to ward off outside invaders that could make you sick. A major player in this system? You might have heard of 'em: **white blood cells**. Some of them, called **phagocytes**, attack germs as they enter your body, and others, called **leukocytes**, recognize previous invaders and strategize about how to attack them. Isn't it awesome that you have a whole staff of security guards in your body ready to protect you?

This system is not a perfect one—obviously we all get sick sometimes. But this is another time your immune system steps in: by helping you get better. We can keep our immune systems functional by eating nutritious foods, getting lots of vitamin C (in things like orange juice), getting enough sleep, and washing our hands. And always be sure to tell an adult when you're feeling crummy. You know your body well and if something feels off, don't hesitate to speak up.

Belly Feeling Good Today? Thank Your Digestive System

Food is one of the most wonderful things about being alive. The salty tang of a pickle, the satisfying crunch of a Granny Smith apple, a gooey chewy piece of pepperoni pizza . . . yummy food is the best. But enjoying flavors and textures of food in your mouth is just the first step of how your body processes all the food you eat and turns it into energy you can use to make your body stronger.

Digestion begins in the mouth. When you chew your food, it mixes with saliva, which helps soften it so it can more easily go down your throat. Saliva also has enzymes, which help break down starches and fats in your food. Once you swallow, the food travels down your throat into your esophagus. The walls of your esophagus create waves to push down the food into your stomach.

The transformation doesn't stop there. Your stomach is a J-shaped sack in your body that keeps mixing and breaking down the food, with more enzymes along with the stomach's gastric juices and powerful muscles. Then, it travels through your small intestine, which isn't very small at all. If you stretched it out, it would be more than 22 feet long! This is where your body finally breaks down the food into stuff your body can use: the juices in your body turn the food in your small intestine into chemicals, which enter your bloodstream, which carries them to your cells, which use those chemicals to help you grow and give you energy. Phew!

And the stuff that can't be broken down? That goes into your large intestine, which slowly pushes it into your colon, and, eventually, out of your body— that's when you need to head to the bathroom (you knew it was all heading there!).

So You're Growing . . . But How, Exactly?

All these parts of your body have been growing and maturing since you were tiny. Did you know that babies have more bones than you do now? Some of our 300 bones fuse together during the growing process, and others harden as they get older. You've been experiencing growth spurts since you were born, and this time of your life is no exception.

You may notice that all of a sudden you tower over everyone in your class. Perhaps your favorite pair of jeans now stop at your ankles or no longer have room for your hips. Or maybe you haven't noticed a growth spurt at all—suddenly you're a lot shorter compared to everyone in your class. This is all normal! People grow at their own pace.

How, exactly, does your body do all this growing? Well, the cells in your body are literally multiplying, and your body is surging with human growth hormone, which is made in a pea-sized organ in your brain called the **pituitary gland**. And a lot of how you grow depends on your family, not your habits. Despite what a well-meaning adult will say about how coffee will stunt your growth or kale will help you shoot up like a weed, height is mostly determined by genes.

And of course, when you hit puberty, other hormones coursing through your body, like estrogen and testosterone, will cause it to grow in other ways. At some point, you'll develop breasts and body hair, and you'll start to smell different. (We'll get into all that later on.)

BODIES THAT WORK
A LITTLE DIFFERENTLY

As you can probably tell by now, the human body is incredibly intricate with one function leading to the next and the next and the—you get it! So, naturally, sometimes things don't work exactly the way they're designed to. When a body does things a little differently, this can lead to certain conditions that people have to treat and manage every day. We'll tell you about some common conditions below. You probably know someone who manages these issues—or maybe you yourself do.

Allergies: An allergy is when your immune system reacts to a foreign substance as if it were dangerous. Chances are, you have some experience with allergies. Allergies come in different forms. Some people have airborne allergies, which means they react to substances in the air, like pollen from trees. Other people are allergic to certain animals, and some people are allergic to certain foods like dairy products or nuts. Some allergies are mild and can be treated with easy-to-find medicines, but others are more severe, and the person must avoid the thing that causes the allergy entirely. So if you have a friend with a peanut allergy, be sure to leave the PB&J at home!

Asthma: This is a lung condition that makes it difficult to breathe. Sometimes asthma is triggered by exercise, allergies, or having a

respiratory illness like a cold or the flu. Most of the time, asthma can be treated with medication. Maybe you know someone who has one of those cool-looking inhalers that makes a *pfft* sound when they press on it.

Diabetes: There are two different types of diabetes. Type 1 diabetes is the type that is most common in kids. This is because it is genetic condition, while type 2 diabetes develops over time and is usually related to lifestyle habits like unhealthy eating. Both types of diabetes have to do with the amount of insulin—the hormone that keeps our blood cells healthy—in a person's body. People with diabetes have to check their insulin levels daily to make sure they're in a typical range, so you might see someone wearing a monitoring device.

You might not be able to see conditions like the ones mentioned above, but people with them are managing them every day.

A Bit About Disabilities

Let's talk a little bit about physical disabilities you can see.

As you know, bodies come in all different shapes and sizes—but they also differ in their abilities. Some people need things like wheelchairs or canes to help them move through the world. Other people might have limb differences, meaning their arms or legs might be shaped differently, or they may not have two arms and two legs. Some people wear devices like hearing aids or cochlear implants to help them hear.

It's normal to notice when a body doesn't look like yours. If you have questions about someone's abilities, feel free to ask your grown-up in private. Being curious is natural, and it's best not to make assumptions. Learning about different disabilities is an excellent way to understand how to be a good friend to that person and to be a more informed, empathetic person overall!

The most important thing to realize is that just because somebody's body might not look like yours (or mine! or hers!), we're all more alike than we are different. We all want to be treated with respect and spoken to with kind words.

LET'S GET READY FOR PUBERTY

Part of growing up means going through the confusing, exciting stage called **puberty**. It could start as young as 8 years old or as late as 13—and the changes can happen in any order. As we discussed in the first chapter, your emotions may be running wild and turning on a dime. But your body is going through a big shift too. So let's get into it.

Your Changing Shape

When you were a little girl, your body shape probably seemed similar to the boys around you. You had a flat chest and your waist might have been pretty much the same width as your hips. When a person assigned female at birth goes through puberty, the extra estrogen (the hormone that is responsible for developing female body parts) in her body often causes her hips to widen. You will probably gain some weight, but your waist may also become smaller compared to your hips. Regardless, you might see curves on your body that you didn't see before.

The reason for all these changes? It is so your body will be prepared to carry a baby one day, if you choose to have one.

Keep this in mind, though: there are all kinds of different body shapes. Not every girl's body will end up looking curvy, and not everyone's waist will get smaller compared to their hips. Some people are shaped like hourglasses, while others are shaped like sticks, apples, pears . . . you get the idea. Not only are all body shapes normal and healthy, but they are also usually determined by what our families look like, not what we eat or how we exercise. And remember, your body is going a little haywire right now. You probably won't know what your adult shape will be for many years. In the meantime, rest assured that your body is doing exactly what it's supposed to be doing: growing!

Your Breasts Will Make Their Appearance

One of the first and most noticeable parts of puberty is that your breasts will start to grow. This'll start to happen gradually, probably between the ages of about 8 and 13 (though a bit earlier or later is completely fine too). First, you'll notice what's called "breast buds"—little mounds under each nipple that may feel tender to the touch. Your nipples might get darker and bigger. As your breasts move through stages of growth, it's quite possible that they'll look pointy, lopsided, or a little wonky. Trust us: this is just part of a very natural process. By the time you reach the end of your teens, your breasts will settle into a more permanent shape—although one may always be a little different than the other, and that's okay too. There are infinite ways for breasts to look: round, teardrop-shaped, oblong, far apart, close together, big, small, firm, soft, and anything in between! All fine, fabulous, and unique to you.

Even if we tell you that all this is normal, it might still feel a little embarrassing to suddenly have these visible lumps under your shirt where you didn't before. And it can be equally nerve-racking if your breasts are taking their sweet time growing.

Puberty is a time when you may become self-conscious and start to compare your body to others, wondering if you, ahem, measure up. You may wonder if your breasts are "too small" or "too big." Despite what kids in school decide is fair game (and there are always a few gossips who think they can weigh in on your changing body), there isn't any such thing as "too" anything.

The fact is, each and every body is on its own time line, so the best we can do is accept what it has in store for us.

You Might Smell Different

Soon your body will be flooded with lots of hormones, which will (among other things) activate the sweat glands in your armpits. This means you'll start to sweat there more than before, and when that sweat mixes with bacteria . . . boom, you have body odor. This new stink is definitely funky—it can smell salty, onion-y, or even a bit like mac 'n' cheese. It's not always pleasant, but again (let's say it together): totally normal!

You May Get Your First Pimples

Those puberty hormones are little multitaskers. They are also busy affecting the oil glands in your body. Oil is essential for healthy hair and skin, but during puberty, it gets the message to produce like crazy. This extra oil tends to mingle with dead skin cells and bacteria. The result? You may notice some new, pesky pimples dotting your once-clear face, back, and chest. *Ugh!* There are few things more annoying than pimples (otherwise known as zits, officially known as acne). But they're often a part of life during this time and for a few years afterward. Most people have to deal with them at some point, even the people who appear to have flawless, glowing complexions. Pimples can show up in different forms:

Blackheads: These tiny, black dots can form when individual pores are clogged but still exposed to air. They're most common on what's called your "T-zone": your forehead, nose, and chin.

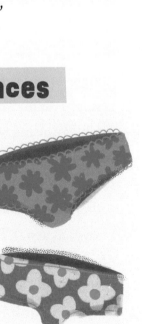

Whiteheads: These are also clogged pores, but they're white because they're closed, so the stuff inside of them doesn't go through the same darkening that happens when it is exposed to oxygen.

Papules or cysts: These are what you might think of as the classic zits or pimples. They're bigger, redder bumps, and often painful to the touch.

You'll Notice Hair in New Places

Your hormones are at it again. This time they're sending messages to your body to produce more hair. And not just anywhere. You'll start to notice some strands growing under your arms and between your legs. The hair that you see down there is called **pubic hair**. This hair might be light and soft at first, and then may get dark, coarse, and curly—although, much like the rest of our bodies, everyone's pubic hair texture and color are different. Your pubic hair might match the color of

the hair on your head, or it might not. And like your breasts, pubic hair growth is usually a long, gradual process. It'll be years before you have the amount you'll have as an adult.

Besides pubic hair, you might also notice that the hairs on your arms and legs are thicker too. The hair on your head might start to get oilier. Or not! We know we're starting to sound like a broken record, but everyone is different. So oily tresses or more hair in other spots on your body may be a big part of puberty for you . . . or you may not notice it at all.

You May See Some Goo in Your Underwear

Did you know your vagina cleans itself? It's true! During puberty, your vagina kicks into high gear and starts producing a clear or milky, mucus-like liquid called **vaginal discharge**. This stuff happens to everyone. It's your body making sure your vagina is clean, moisturized, and infection-free.

This discharge shouldn't smell like much. If it does, particularly if the smell is *bad*, tell a parent. This is a sign of possible infection, so you should head to the doctor.

YOU'LL GET YOUR PERIOD

At some point, after you've noticed some of the changes we've already talked about (and especially if you've noticed vaginal discharge), your body will reach a *big*, important milestone: you'll start bleeding from your vagina for a few days to a week every month. This is called **menstruation**, or, more casually, "getting your period." The average age for starting your period is around 12, though it might happen as early as 9 or 10, or as late as 14 or 15.

It may not exactly sound appealing. Blood? *From my vagina?* We'll admit, these few days aren't always the most comfortable or convenient. But while blood is usually a sign that we're hurt or that something is wrong, the beautiful thing about periods is that they're a signal of your body working exactly as it should. And it means that your body is gearing up to one day have a baby, when and if you're ready.

Okay, let's back up. Why exactly do we bleed every month? It all starts with your uterus, the place where your body would grow a fertilized egg that could eventually become a baby. All month, thanks to your hormones, your uterus will prepare for this possibility by lining its walls with blood. When there is no fertilized egg in the uterus (and therefore no fetus), the lining breaks down and flows through your vagina. That's it! That's your period.

Period blood doesn't look the same as the blood you see when you cut yourself or skin your knee—it

can be darker and have more of a molasses-like texture, maybe with little clumps here and there. It might look more brown than red on light days. Your flow can be unpredictable at first, but it usually settles into a pattern eventually. A common cycle might start out with a heavier flow and then taper off after a few days.

What to Expect from Your First Period

The first time you bleed can look all kinds of ways, and it may or may not be the whole enchilada of a weeklong flow. It could be as simple as a smear of brownish red on your underwear. It could mean that you'll be having it monthly from now on, but more likely it'll take a while (sometimes a couple of years) for your periods to become regular. Many girls find that, after the first time, their periods disappear for a few months before they return.

So what if you go to the bathroom and see this telltale smear (or drip or gush)? Don't panic! You may feel a bit bashful or even ashamed, but there's no reason to be embarrassed. Some families openly celebrate this moment, and why shouldn't they? It's exciting! The menstrual cycle has enabled the birth of almost every single person on planet Earth. How cool is that?

Still, you're bleeding, so you do need to spring into action. If your period comes as a surprise, and you don't have any supplies with you, your first order of business should be to fold up a few squares of toilet paper and put them in your underwear to soak up the blood. Chances are you probably *won't* leak all the way to your outside clothes, but if you do, try to reach for the nearest jacket or sweater to tie around your waist. Then tell an older woman you trust that you've started your period. We guarantee that she'll recall exactly how this felt and help you find the things you need ASAP. Speaking of . . .

Tampons, Pads, and Other Products

One of the first issues you'll have to tackle when you get your period is how to catch the blood so it doesn't stain your clothes. The two most common options for dealing with the blood are pads and tampons. There's also absorbent period underwear, where you bleed right into the cloth—some even come in cute prints especially for girls your age. Those are better for the environment than pads, but they require a little cleaning effort. Finally, there are menstrual cups and menstrual discs, which are usually reusable and last longer than tampons. They take a while to get the hang of, though, so you may want to start with a more basic method.

Most girls wear pads at first, since they're the easiest to use. So let's talk about them. Pads are rectangle-shaped and made of thick, super-absorbent material. They come with a sticky side that goes directly onto your underwear, and some have "wings" that fold over the edges of your underwear to make extra-sure there aren't leaks. You'll need to peel off a thin layer of paper to expose the sticky side that adheres to your underwear. There are pads for all stages of your period, from the lightest to heaviest flow.

WHAT THE REBELS SAY

"We are all imperfectly beautiful, so let's embrace that."
—Lili Reinhart, actor

100

Types of Pads

* Overnight (the thickest and most absorbent)
* Maxi (thick and very absorbent, for the absolute heaviest flow)
* Super (for continuous, still kinda heavy days)
* Regular (thinner, but they still soak up lots, for medium flow)
* Thin/Ultra Thin (for lighter flow days)
* Panty Liners (for trickles and spotting)

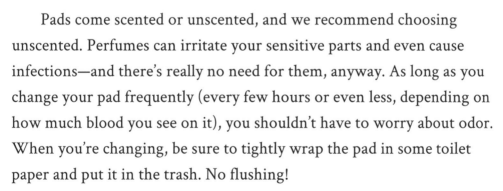

Pads come scented or unscented, and we recommend choosing unscented. Perfumes can irritate your sensitive parts and even cause infections—and there's really no need for them, anyway. As long as you change your pad frequently (every few hours or even less, depending on how much blood you see on it), you shouldn't have to worry about odor. When you're changing, be sure to tightly wrap the pad in some toilet paper and put it in the trash. No flushing!

What about tampons? They're definitely a bit more involved than just sticking a pad to your underpants. Tampons are tightly packed tubes of absorbent material that fit inside your vagina, often with the help of a cardboard or plastic applicator. They catch the blood before it reaches the outside of your body. The muscles in your vagina hold up the tampon, so don't worry—it won't fall out! Many girls love the convenience and comfort of tampons. When they're in right, you shouldn't feel them at all, and they make things like swimming and playing sports a lot easier during your period. But if you're not used to it, sticking something up there might seem scary or awkward, so take your time. Tampons will be there if and when you decide to use them.

When you do, set aside a little time in the bathroom to practice, practice, practice. Most girls find that a smaller-sized tampon (often called "slim" or "junior") is more comfortable at first. There are usually detailed instructions on the package about how to use the applicator and suggested positions to try in the bathroom in order to get the most comfortable fit. All tampons are a bit different, but here's a bit of info for the tampon newbie: there's a little bagel-shaped piece of tissue the size of a dime, called the "cervix," blocking the opening of the uterus, and the hole in the center is really tiny. So tampons can never, ever get lost inside you. That means the tampon is probably supposed to be in a little deeper than you might think!

Picture This:

Chloe was a week into her first summer at sleepaway camp when she woke up in the middle of the night feeling some cramping in her lower tummy. She headed to the bathroom with her flashlight. Sure enough, there was a streak of blood on her underwear. She'd gotten her first period.

Chloe could have panicked, but luckily she already had a plan in place. A few weeks ago, before she headed off to camp, she and her aunt bought a cute travel case with palm trees on it and put together an emergency period kit for her to bring to camp. In the travel case, they included: an assortment of pads, an extra pair of dark underwear, a plastic baggie for blood-stained underwear, a travel-size pack of baby wipes, and a mini package of M&MS (Chloe's favorite)—this is exciting, so treats are in order!

Chloe tiptoed back to her bunk and grabbed the toiletry case. In it, there was everything she needed—including a sweet surprise note that her aunt had slipped in at the last minute. Later that summer, when another girl in her bunk was caught by surprise by her period, Chloe knew just what to do. She slipped her one of the pads from the emergency kit.

One of the great things about getting your period—it's not only a major step of growing up, but it also inducts you into the "supply sisterhood" of being able to help out when another girl is in a jam!

What Your Period Might Feel Like

Listen, your period is incredible and nothing to be ashamed of, but it can also be a major pain. Sometimes literally. Period cramps are definitely a thing! It's hard to describe how they feel unless you've experienced them. They're usually more of a dull, constant ache than a sharp pain, but they can be intense. Not only that, but you may also feel more tired or sensitive during your period. That's why it's essential to come up with ways your body can feel comfier for that week or so.

Once you've had your period for a few months in a row, pay close attention to your particular flow. Take a warm bath or invest in a heating pad to soothe cramps. Build in time to take it easy and munch on your favorite treats. (Fun fact: the magnesium in chocolate actually might help your muscles relax!) Take a walk in the fresh air to energize you. If none of that helps, ask your grown-up about taking medicine, such as ibuprofen. And don't be afraid to speak to your grown-ups or doctor if you're in a *lot* of pain. Periods aren't fun, but pain that doesn't ease with mild painkillers could mean there's a more serious problem.

That Pesky Thing Called "PMS"

PMS—or "premenstrual syndrome"—is a collection of symptoms that might show up in the week or so before your period. (Once again, you can thank your hormones.) There are a ton of these symptoms, so here goes: you may feel bloated, tired, and headachy. You could feel constipated, or you could have a bit of diarrhea. Perhaps you'll crave sugar or salty foods. Your breasts or lower back might feel sore. You might notice more pimples than usual. You may also feel more emotional, anxious, weepy, or quick to anger during this time. The list goes on and on! Years ago, PMS symptoms weren't taken seriously by doctors, and there was even a myth that they didn't exist at all. Nowadays, though, it's generally accepted that PMS does exist, and even that there's a particularly intense form of it, called "premenstrual dysphoric disorder" (PMDD). Again, if any of these symptoms feel like they're a little too much or too intrusive in your life, don't be afraid to speak up.

TAKING CARE OF YOUR NEW BODY

Now you know all about the changes your body is about to go through. Not all of them are going to feel awesome, and some of them might require you to give your body a little extra TLC. Here's your road map to feeling and looking your freshest.

Protecting Your Skin

We talked about the different kinds of pimples you might be noticing on your face—all annoying, all here to ruin your day! Your first impulse might be to go on the offensive and buy every acne product in the skin-care aisle. This is exactly what you should *not* do. Mystery potions with lots of ingredients can cause skin to freak out and get even worse. An occasional face mask or yummy-smelling lotion is fine for fun, but the best thing you can do for your skin is wash it with a gentle cleanser and top it off with a few drops of an oil-free moisturizer. (Yes, even if you have oily skin—skipping moisturizer can tell your face to produce even more oil, worsening the problem.)

If your skin gets shiny throughout the day, it can be nice to reach for some oil-blotting sheets in your backpack. They're a quick and cheap way to freshen up.

Whatever you do, don't pick at or pop your pimples. It can leave scars or make a zit look worse. And it can hurt a lot!

There *are* a couple of products that can help mild acne. Look for creams with benzoyl peroxide (which kills bacteria) or toners with salicylic acid (which helps clean off dead skin cells). These drugstore products work best on mild or moderate breakouts. More serious acne is really the job for a doctor called a **dermatologist**. If you feel like your acne is getting in the way of you feeling confident and happy, talk to your grown-ups about making an appointment.

One more word about protecting your skin: you must, must, must use sunscreen! Chances are your grown-ups chased you around with a big sticky bottle of the stuff at the beach when you were smaller. Now it's your turn to take care of your own skin to prevent sunburn and skin cancer. (Not to mention wrinkles later on.) Sunscreen comes in all kinds of skin-friendly versions, like oil-free, face-sensitive, and spray-on. It's sometimes even included in face moisturizer, so you don't have to think about an extra step. It might be tough to think about a future you with sun damage, but take it from us: your skin will thank you later!

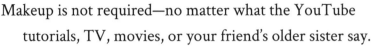

Makeup is not required—no matter what the YouTube tutorials, TV, movies, or your friend's older sister say. If you do decide to try it, remember that it's a way to have fun, accentuate your already gorgeous features, and express your creativity. It's not about "fixing" imperfections or keeping up with anyone at school. Think of makeup as a way to express your individuality, rather than to be like everyone else. And of course, if covering up that pimple on Picture Day will make you feel more confident, go for it! But remember, your face is 100 percent lovely just the way it is.

That said, makeup can be a blast to experiment with. It's up to you what look to go for (and, we're sorry to tell you, your parents might have a say in the matter), but our advice is to start slow. Try your hand at some tinted moisturizers, lip glosses, skin highlighters, and clear mascara. Big, bold colors might be too much too quickly, and foundation or powder might aggravate your sensitive skin. It also depends on where you are going. Things like glitter or electric-blue eyeliner might be fun for, say, sleepovers, but not school.

And finally, no matter how tired you feel, remember to wash your face and remove your makeup before bed!

Come Up Smelling Like Roses

Okay, obviously smelling like an actual flower all the time is impossible. But since puberty does mean we'll start to sweat more and therefore smell more too, you might want to start thinking about ways to freshen up. Step one: especially after your underarms start to have hair, take a few seconds to lather up those areas in the shower. Then, you could consider using a deodorant and/or an antiperspirant, which do different things (but are often combined into one product). **Deodorant** covers up the scent of body odor, either with other fragrances or with neutral fresheners like baking soda. **Antiperspirant** prevents or decreases how much you sweat by temporarily blocking the pores sweat comes out of.

Finding a deodorant that works for you might take some trial and error, especially when it comes to "your" scent. Also, it's not strictly required to wear deodorant at all, as long as you're making an effort to keep your pits clean.

Air It Out Down There

You might also start to sweat more between your legs than you used to (and, as we mentioned earlier, you could also notice some discharge in your underwear). Any moisture is heaven for bacteria and fungi that can cause stink or infections. So it's important to keep your crotch clean and dry too. Avoid putting soap *inside* your labia or vagina—it could upset the delicate balance of chemicals in that area—but be sure to suds up any pubic hair and the creases between your thighs and pelvis. Cotton underwear is the most breathable choice, so stick to that. And try to change out of your bathing suit in a timely fashion. Staying in wet clothes can cause rashes or an itchy, uncomfortable condition called a **yeast infection**.

Do I Need to Do Something About My Leg Hair?

Nope! You certainly don't need to remove your hair if you don't want to. It's becoming more and more common to go au naturel. But if you'd prefer to try a smooth look, there's no health-related reason why you shouldn't go ahead and try it. Just make sure to ask your grown-up first.

The most common way to remove the hair on your legs is to shave it. There's also waxing, which can be painful and expensive, and hair removal creams that dissolve the hair, which are pain-free but often smelly and not cheap, either. Let's focus on shaving for now, since it's the easiest method for a beginner. Here are some things to know.

Shaving is a commitment. A couple of days after shaving, your legs will feel a bit coarse and prickly with what's called "stubble." It happens when hair is bluntly cut by a razor, and it means that you'll have to routinely shave in order to keep that silky feel. So make sure you're prepared to keep shaving, or at least have a week or two of the rough stuff on your legs.

Shaving isn't without its "ouch" moments. A razor can create irritated red bumps, called "razor burn," if it's not helped along with a sufficiently slippery goo like shaving cream or lotion. Also, when dragged the wrong way, it's possible to cut or nick yourself with a razor. So proceed with caution.

All razors are not created equal. There are disposable razors that you throw away after a few uses and permanent razors with blades you replace. There are single-blade razors and double-blade razors and even triple-blade razors. There are also razors that are marketed to girls, but they're really not all that different from the razors men use to shave their faces—besides maybe being a pretty color or a stylish shape.

Disposable razors are cheap, but replaceable razors are better for the environment. Whichever kind you choose, make sure the razors are new and sharp—or else you risk nicking yourself. Though their shave is not quite as close as double- or triple-blade razors, single-blade razors are probably best for beginners, since they're less likely to cut your legs.

A Step-by-Step Shaving Guide

1. **Get a bowl of warm water and a wet washcloth and bring them to an empty bathtub.** When you become a shaving master, you might be able to quickly shave in the shower. But for your first time, it helps to be on dry land.

2. **Wet your legs and apply a rich shaving cream, gel, or lotion.** Regular old hair conditioner works great too—anything that will coat your legs with moisture and will stay put during the shaving process. Some girls have noticeable hair only up to their knees so they coat only that part, while others will lather up their whole leg. It's up to you!

3. **Start at your ankle and work your way up.** The key here is to shave against your hair's natural growth pattern to get the closest shave. And remember to be as gentle as possible—pressing too hard can cause cuts and irritation.

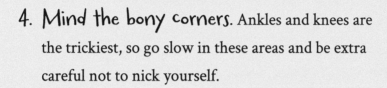

4. **Mind the bony corners.** Ankles and knees are the trickiest, so go slow in these areas and be extra careful not to nick yourself.

5. **Rinse out your razor in the bowl of warm water after one or two strokes.** Depending on how much hair you have, you may not have to clean the razor *every* time. But the less clogged it is, the better the results.

6. **When you're done, wash off your legs.** You can do this with the wet washcloth or the tub's spout, depending on how much extra shaving cream there is.

7. **Wait for the lotion!** Your skin might be a bit sensitive, so hold off on applying any lotion or oil for an hour or so after shaving.

And . . . you're done! Enjoy the silky smoothness.

Buying Your First Bra

If a bra sounds like something you want to try, talk it over with your grown-up first and discuss what bra you might like to get. This first shopping trip might be a little awkward, but it can also be kind of fun, in the way shopping for any clothes can be. Bras come in all kinds of shapes, sizes, and patterns. Some girls opt for a playful hot-pink or polka-dot bra, while others prefer to buy one in white or in a color closer to their skin tone so it's invisible under a shirt.

Here are some introductory bras you might consider on your very first shopping trip.

Tank tops and camisoles: While not technically bras, buying one of these could allow you to test out the feel of wearing something stretchy under your shirt without fully committing to Being a Bra-Wearer.

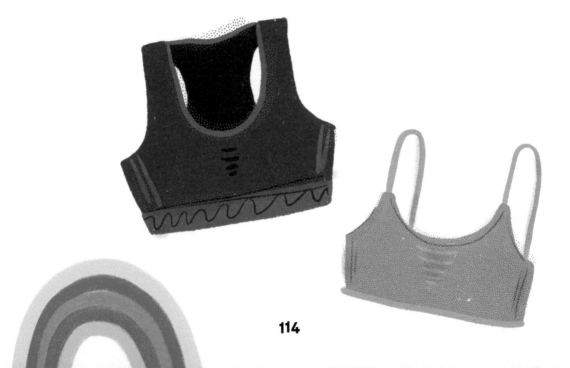

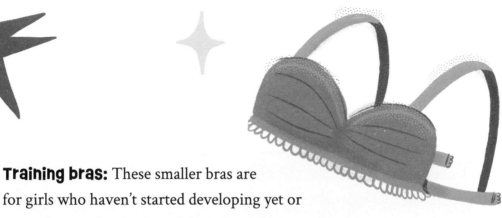

Training bras: These smaller bras are for girls who haven't started developing yet or are at the very beginning of their development. They're soft and stretchy and usually you just pull them over your head—no tricky clasps or anything. They don't really "train" your breasts for anything, but it could help *you* get used to the idea of wearing a bra. It all comes down to confidence and comfort. If a training bra will do that for you, go for it!

Sports bras and bralettes: These are stretchy, tight bras that feel a bit like tank tops, only they don't cover your stomach. Some of these have adjustable straps for a nice, snug fit, but they're generally made of one continuous piece of fabric—not many seams or hooks.

Once your breasts get a little bigger, you might think about getting measured. An ill-fitting bra is truly a tragic experience. Not only can it make your chest look lumpy and misshapen, but it can also be monumentally uncomfortable! Fitted bra sizes have both a letter and a number, like 34A or 36D. The letters represent your cup size. The cups are the parts that cover your breasts. A is smallest, and the cup sizes go up from there. The numbers represent inches, and they're the circumference of your rib cage right under your breasts (or your "band size").

Many stores have a special salesperson who will help you figure out your size. This might sound like the most mortifying thing on Earth—*a stranger measuring my breasts??*—but this person has seen it all. It only takes a couple minutes, and they'll be able to ensure you have a perfect fit. You can also measure at home if that's more your speed.

For your band size: Without wearing a bra or shirt, take a soft or cloth tape measure and wrap it around your back and under your breasts, where a bra would normally sit—not too tight and not too loose, exactly how you'd like the band of a bra to fit. If you get an even number, that's your band size. Round up if you get an odd number.

For your cup size: Wear a bra if you already have one, so that your breasts are in the place you want them to be. (If you don't have one, unadorned breasts are fine.) Take the same soft tape measure and wrap it around the fullest part of your chest, usually on top of the nipple. Then subtract your band size from this number. *Voilà!* The difference is your cup size. 0=AA, 1=A, 2=B, 3=C, and so on.

HAIR TIPS

Puberty can change the hair on your head without warning. A surge in estrogen can make your hair thicker and glossier, or the wavy hair you've had since you were a child can suddenly turn into tight curls. No matter what texture you have, it's yours and it's awesome. But now that you're largely caring for your own body (and since no one likes a bad hair day), it's worth taking a little time and getting to know what's good for your hair type.

In our experience, too many products can make hair look dull or oily. (And they can get expensive!) So, we found one secret weapon for your hair type that will keep your tresses looking fabulous.

Hair Type: Fine and Straight
Secret Weapon: Dry shampoo. It adds a nice texture to thin hair, and it can help dry out any excess oil between washings.

Hair Type: Thick and Straight
Secret Weapon: A few drops of oil or serum. Your hair can soak up just about anything, so just a little bit of gloss will make it look shiny and healthy.

Hair Type: Wavy
Secret Weapon: Sea-salt spray. A spritz or two of beachy salt spray can make waves look more defined.

Hair Type: Fine and Curly
Secret Weapon: Sulfate-free conditioner. It'll keep frizz to a minimum without weighing down your hair.

Hair Type: Coarse and Curly
Secret Weapon: Curl cream (or a spot of conditioner in a pinch). Your hair needs moisture, but it can also need some help staying bouncy. Curl cream does both!

Hair Type: Coily
Secret Weapon: Deep conditioner or hair mask. Tightly coiled hair can get dry easily, so invest in a rich, creamy conditioner and leave it on for 20 minutes before washing out.

BEING IN AWE OF YOUR BODY

Even though you might understand that all these body shifts are natural and expected, it can still be a struggle sometimes to accept this new skin you're in. It doesn't help that just as you're going through monumental changes, it seems that people at school and on the internet will have a lot of opinions about how thin or curvy to be, what clothes are in style, and what hairstyles are cutest.

The best advice we can give you to block out all this noise is this: focus on what your body can *do* instead of obsessing over what it looks like. Have you noticed that your times at track practice have gotten better after you sprouted a few inches? Take a second to thank those growing bones. Are you usually the person in your household to dodge that seasonal cold? Be proud of your immune system. Were you the person with the most resolve and endurance on that group hike you just took? It's a wonderful thing when your heart, lungs, and muscles rise to the occasion. Your body has been with you through thick and thin—be kind to it, rather than criticize it.

You may have heard messages like "every body is beautiful" or "love your body no matter what." These sentiments mean well, and of course it would be lovely to feel 100 percent positive about your body 100 percent of the time—and maybe you do! If that's the case, feel free to skip this section. That kind of confidence is amazing, inspiring, and deserves to be celebrated. But

WHAT THE REBELS SAY

"It doesn't really matter how you look in pictures. It just matters that you're there."
—Megan Jayne Crabbe, body-positivity advocate

119

for some of us, feeling cool with our appearance all of the time isn't realistic. It's okay to get a little frustrated with your body or feel a bit awkward about its changes. For some people, something called **body neutrality** is more useful than body positivity. Body neutrality doesn't mandate constant love of our bodies so much as respect for how hard they work for us every single day. Besides, beauty isn't the most important thing in the world.

Your value shouldn't be tied to how you look.

Try to focus on things like your intelligence, your empathy, your sense of humor, your strength—not whether you're judged as beautiful by the outside world.

Picture This:

For as long as she could remember, Ellie was one of the shortest and thinnest girls in her class and on her swim team. But over the summer, she suddenly grew several inches and her once-lean frame now had curves where there weren't any before. Ellie didn't feel totally comfortable in this new body. She felt like people stared at her at the pool, and she had to get all new clothes.

But one day, Ellie started to appreciate her body in a completely new way. It all happened at her first big swim meet of the year. As she waited at the edge of the pool, crouched on her starting block, she felt her familiar self-consciousness. She adjusted her swimsuit for the thousandth time. It felt like all eyes were on her. But when the starting horn went off, she forgot all about her new insecurities. It was just her and the pool. She noticed that she was stronger than she thought—certainly stronger than she was last year, before her growth spurt. Her legs were pushing her faster, her arms were stretching farther, and her lungs were lasting longer without breaths.

When she reached the touchpad and brought her head up from the water to look at her time, she was stunned. She shaved a whole five seconds off her 100-meter freestyle! It was then that she realized those extra inches aren't so bad. After that incredible swim meet, she kept noticing more amazing changes. She could reach the high shelf in her kitchen. She could more easily lift her little sister. Pretty soon, she stopped wishing she could go back to her little-girl body. Instead, she started to really embrace and appreciate all the new things her body could do!

Evaluate What You See on TV and the Internet

No matter how committed you are to not thinking or talking negatively about your body, it can be hard in the face of the images we see every day on our phones and TV. The seemingly perfect bodies and faces of movie stars, influencers, and models can threaten to erase all the good stuff we know about our own regular bodies. These people are literally paid to spend lots of time on their looks and their bodies, sometimes in ways that are unhealthy. And many of the images we see of these professional beautiful people aren't even real—many of them have been edited using a program like Photoshop, where someone can take a picture of a person and whiten their teeth, make their legs or waist thinner . . . the list goes on. Actor Lili Reinhart has been outspoken about how social media can make us feel bad about ourselves. She has said, "Do not set impossible goals of meeting those fake standards. It's unrealistic to think that your body or my body will ever look like anyone else's. That's not the way it's supposed to be. We are all imperfectly beautiful."

There have been studies showing that social media can hurt teen girls' mental health. So if you're someone who uses Instagram, TikTok, or other platforms, it's important to take breaks from scrolling if you sense any negative emotions coming up. Remind yourself often that those images aren't real life. Support brands like Aerie and Dove that vow not to Photoshop the people in their advertisements. Feel free to immediately unfollow any accounts that make you feel down on yourself. Replace them with accounts that explicitly and joyfully celebrate the strength and power of the human body, such as body-positivity advocate Megan Jayne Crabbe.

How to Spot a Photoshopped Picture

One way to explode unrealistic expectations of yourself is to know when a photo has been edited up the wazoo. Examine the image carefully.

Signs an Image Has Been Edited

* Bent edges or liquidy-looking shapes
* Objects in the background that seem out of place or off
* Uneven color on someone's face or body
* Wildly out-of-proportion body parts
* Missing shadows or contours
* Impossibly creamy skin (everyone has pores!)

If you notice any of these things, then chances are the picture has been edited! Start thinking of these images as bizarre arts-and-crafts projects, not images with which to compare yourself. They simply do not reflect the reality of the human body.

Quick Ways to Feel Empowered!

Let's face it we all have some low moments here and there. When this happens, take a minute to be present with your body and comfort yourself. Here are a few ideas.

Body appreciation mantras: A mantra is a statement that you say or think that helps boost your confidence. Make a list of positive statements and set them aside for times when your confidence falters. An example of these might be:

My body is unbelievably powerful.
My body knows just what to do, every minute of every day.
I'm growing and changing, and that's wonderful.

Giving thanks: Grab a pen and a piece of paper and literally thank your body for things it did for you today. This list could look something like this:

Thank you, reflexes, for protecting me from being burned on the stove today.

Thank you, nose, for sneezing out that dust this morning.

Thank you, tongue, for making it possible to taste that delicious smoothie after volleyball practice!

Power poses: Sometimes moving your body into a shape that gets your blood pumping and stretches your muscles can ground you in the moment and remind you of your strength. Examples of those could be:

Head high, feet wide, and hands on hips
Back arched, hands high and wide
One knee bent forward, two hands
outstretched (like you're about to give
a hug)

Text an empowerment buddy: Come up with a code word with your most positive, encouraging friend that basically means "I need a reminder of how strong and capable I am." The code word can be anything: something random like "macaroni" or something reassuring like "gut check."

Mindful Break

Scan the code to learn a calming and empowering relaxation technique.

Your Body Is Your Own

So now you know that it's a wonderful feeling to have the utmost respect for your body. Guess what? You can also insist that everybody else respects your body too—and your boundaries. Consent means that you get to decide what happens to your body and who gets to touch it. Yes, even your parents and the other adults in your life. When someone goes in for a hug and you're not feeling it, just say, "I'd prefer a high five today." If someone ever touches you in a way that doesn't feel good, you should feel free to say so. If you don't feel comfortable telling that person in the moment, let your grown-up know.

This also means, of course, that you need permission from your friends or anyone else if you want to touch them in any way. This doesn't always mean waiting for an explicit yes or no. It's also a good idea to be in tune with others' body language. If you notice a friend looking uncomfortable or backing away from your touch, take that as a sign that they probably don't want to be touched. When you meet someone, you can also straight-up ask them, "Do you do hugs or high fives?" It's a super easy way to find out what someone is comfortable with!

GET MOVING!

What comes to mind when someone says "exercise"? Is it a treadmill at the gym, a soccer game, swim lessons, weights, a stretchy yoga class, or a hike? The answer is, of course, all of the above! As long as your muscles are working and your heart is beating faster than normal, whatever you're doing counts as exercise, which is awesome. Even though it's not always that easy to motivate yourself, almost everyone can admit that *having done exercise* is a fabulous feeling.

Why wouldn't it be? Moving your body is all-around great for you. It strengthens your muscles, including that muscle in the middle of your chest: your heart. Somehow it gives you more energy *and* makes it easier to sleep at night. A win-win!

Not only is it good for your body, but it also works wonders for your mind. Getting your heart rate up increases blood flow to your brain and helps your brain grow new blood vessels. Exercising releases chemicals called **neurotrophins**, which improve your memory and learning ability. (You might wanna do a few jumping jacks between study sessions!)

And as we mentioned in Chapter 1, working out can be a lifesaver when your moods feel out of your control. When you exercise, your body is flooded with **endorphins**, which is your body's homegrown way of relieving stress

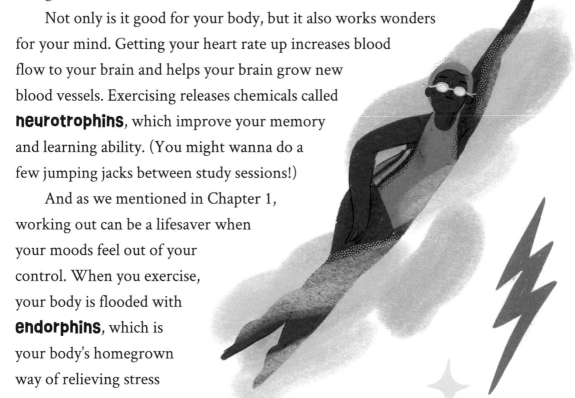

and depression. It can be a way to let off some steam if you're angry, distract yourself if you're having obsessive thoughts, or feel good about your body's strength if you're feeling negatively about how you look. Exercise isn't a magic solution to all your problems, but it really can make you feel good about yourself in lots of ways.

Everyday Exercise

Look, relaxing is awesome. We don't blame you if you're not used to moving your body regularly and you're afraid to begin a routine. But you don't have to be on a sports team or have good coordination to go out and exercise. Don't worry—you can start small and low-key! Nobody has to train for a marathon, now or ever. Here are some simple ways to get your blood pumping.

Take a walk instead of asking for a ride. It's that simple! This is the most basic, natural way for humans to get around, and even though it might not *feel* like fitness, it most certainly is. You're working your leg and butt muscles just by walking. And if you walk briskly, your heart rate will creep up. Walking is a fantastic way to clear your head and get some sunshine on your face—but it's legitimate exercise too.

Or take a dog for a walk. Does walking seem a little . . . pointless? Take a dog! That will give your walk a purpose and a healthy pace—most dogs like to keep it moving. If you don't have a dog, offer to walk your busy neighbor's dog. They'll be happy they don't have to pay a dog walker.

Play with your own weight. You don't need any fancy equipment to put some resistance on your muscles. All you need is your own body. Find a rug or a towel and do a few squats, lunges, sit-ups, and push-ups. You can even do standing push-ups by pushing your arms against a wall. If that feels okay, do a few more. No pressure!

Bike around your neighborhood. Biking is a wonderful way to strengthen your leg muscles and get your heart rate up. It's also a lot of fun! Gliding down hills, feeling the wind in your hair and the sun on your face—what could be better? You can also get a group together and bike to the shops to grab a lemonade or refreshing drink after all your hard work.

Learn a few yoga stretches. Yoga is a form of exercise that not only stretches and flexes your muscles, but can also help along mindfulness, body acceptance, and relaxation. There are lots of YouTube videos that will break down the basics of sun salutations for beginners.

Throw a dance party! Dancing is a great way to move your body because you can do it pretty much anywhere, either solo or in a group. Maybe you just want to play your favorite song in your bedroom and jump around. Or perhaps you and your bestie can learn that new dance that's been blowing up online!

WHAT THE REBELS SAY

"On the first day of basketball, I tried, and I didn't enjoy it at all. But I kept playing, and overall, I had fun playing with my friends."
—Ellie H., 10, California, USA

When You're Exercising, Don't Forget To . . .

Drink lots of water. Hydration is important when you're sweating and working your muscles.

Stretch before you go. Getting a cramp when you're on a roll is super annoying, so warm up first.

Listen to your body. If it feels like too much at any point, stop. If you're in pain, stop. If you're exhausted and out of breath but feel like you "should" keep going so you can reach your goal, you should probably stop. Exercise can be a challenge, but it shouldn't be a punishment.

It's Exercise Time! What's Your Next Move?

1. The weather is perfect! What are you doing out in the sunshine?

A. Taking my dog for a walk on a nature trail

B. Grabbing my skateboard and heading to the skate park

C. Meeting up at the basketball court with my team

D. Organizing a game of capture the flag with the neighborhood kids

2. Homework break! How would you get your energy out?

A. Run around the yard barefoot—it feels so good to go outside after being cooped up!

B. Go for a quick bike ride around the block

C. Practice some volleyball drills so I'm ready for my next game

D. Turn up the tunes for an impromptu dance party!

3. It's show-and-tell day at school. What do you bring in?

A. My seashell collection

B. My new roller skates

C. A scrapbook I made full of pictures of my friends

D. The souvenir I got on a recent family trip

4. If you could learn one new physical activity, what would it be?

A. Rock climbing! I'd love to scale tall mountains one day.

B. Mountain biking through winding trails

C. Tennis. I want to play as well as the pros.

D. A backflip—now that's a cool party trick!

5. Dinnertime! You're helping make a new recipe—what's your favorite part of cooking?

A. Taste testing!
B. Using the food processor
C. Eating the dish with friends and family
D. Stirring ingredients, kneading dough, or cracking eggs

6. You're at a state park with lots of activities. What's first on your list?

A. Picking blueberries in the bushes
B. Waterskiing on the lake
C. Playing softball with my friends
D. The zipline, for sure!

7. What is most likely to be part of your evening routine?

A. An after-dinner walk outside
B. Watching my favorite athlete on TV or YouTube
C. Making sure my sports uniform is clean for the next day
D. Reading . . . or coloring . . . or listening to music. I change it up!

Answers

MOSTLY As: ONE WITH NATURE

To you, exercise is synonymous with getting outside. Find your closest nature reserve or state park and explore with your friends and grown-ups. You'll love moving your body and feeling the fresh air on your skin.

MOSTLY Bs: HOT WHEELS

To you, exercise should be fast and fun! You love jumping on your bike and zooming around your neighborhood. For your next birthday, try heading to a roller rink! You'll have a blast dance-skating with your friends.

MOSTLY Cs: GO TEAM!

Your weekends are packed with practices and games, and you love the camaraderie of being part of a team. Next time you have a free afternoon, coordinate a backyard badminton tournament!

MOSTLY Ds: CHANGE IT UP!

You love to move, but you don't have one particular exercise you always do. That's great—mixing it up makes it so you're never bored! Have you ever tried Zumba? You'd love the fast-paced, spontaneous nature of this dance workout.

133

FEEDING AND FUELING YOUR BODY

We hear a lot about "healthy foods," but not everyone—not even doctors—always agrees about what that is. The bottom line is that some foods, like candy or snacks, with lots of oil, fat, sugar, or salt, are packed with empty calories and don't really nourish your body. Others have what food scientists call "nutritional value"—they have lots of vitamins and minerals, or whole grains and proteins. But that doesn't necessarily mean you should *never* have empty calories or *only* have extremely nutritious foods. Let's look at a few basic truths that most people can agree on.

Eat lots of fruits and veggies. You can't have too many of these. Fruits and veggies are often loaded with vitamins you need to grow, as well as fiber, which helps your digestive system be more regular—that means going number two every day or almost every day.

Variety and moderation are key. Pretty much everything is fine to eat, as long as it's not the *only* thing you eat. And as a general rule, you should eat more nutritious things than non-nutritious things. For example, having a handful of berries is great, but a handful of cookies is probably not the best choice—stick to one or two. Eating a balanced diet will make sure you get all the nutrition you need, but it'll still allow you to enjoy a wide variety of foods. A simple rule of thumb is to have a colorful plate at every meal.

Give your body fuel throughout the day.
Eating a good breakfast before school helps you stay alert during class. A big nutritious lunch helps you avoid a four o'clock slump. And a healthy dinner sets you up for a solid night's sleep. A couple of snacks mixed into your day is fine too. You're growing at a speedy rate, so you need to refuel!

Listen to when your body says "I'm hungry" and "I'm full." There's no hard-and-fast rule about how much to eat, so it's best to just go by your own stomach's cues. Pro tip: it takes about 20 minutes for your brain to register how much food is in your stomach. So if possible, having a leisurely meal is best.

Pay attention to what foods make your body feel good. What meals leave you the most energized? What makes you feel slow and tired? Does your tummy hurt after eating certain foods? Starting to tune into how you react to foods is key to a healthy body.

When Food and Exercise Take Over Your Brain

Being conscientious about your health and how your body feels is usually a good thing. However, sometimes people pay *too* much attention to diet and fitness—to the point where it starts to threaten their mental and physical health. While this is a time in your life when you need lots of healthy food to grow, it's also a time when you may start to be more conscious of how your body looks to others. Add in a culture that's obsessed with losing weight and looking "perfect," and our relationship to food and exercise can get pretty messed up. Which is such a shame because they are wonderful things on their own!

Here's the thing: diets that promise magic results and lots of weight loss are very, very unlikely to work. And they're often not healthy. So they end up being a waste of time. Why count calories when you could be reading a good book, going on a bike ride, or hanging out with your friends?

Right now, your body and brain need all the nutrients they can get! Rather than worrying about every morsel you eat, it's best to take care of your body as best you can and accept its little imperfections. The things you don't like about your body now, you might love in a few years—that happens all the time!

Eating Disorders and How to Spot Them

We can tell you not to obsess about weight until the cows come home, but we also know that, for some people, it's easier said than done. Sometimes, worries over food and exercise can become a full-blown eating disorder. Disorders like **anorexia** (which involves serious restriction of food and fear of gaining weight) or **bulimia** (which is when someone binges food and then throws it up) can negatively affect your heart, bones, teeth, digestive system, and more.

The good news is that eating disorders can be treated—but only if they're noticed. Not everyone who has an eating disorder is very thin or obvious about their behavior.

Here are a few questions to ask if you suspect that either you or someone you love has an eating disorder.

Do You or Does Your Loved One . . .

* skip meals?

* focus on and complain relentlessly about food, calories, portions, and exercise?

* seem to have lost a dramatic amount of weight in a short time?

* constantly say you/they feel or look fat?

* make excuses for not eating?

* eat in private or act secretive about food?

* seem to excessively exercise?

* often leave during or after a meal to use the bathroom?

* have rituals attached to meals, like chopping up food into tiny pieces?

If the answers to any of these questions are "yes," it may be a sign of disordered eating. It can be really, really hard to approach a friend whom you suspect might have an eating disorder. Often, secretiveness is a big part of it, and they may deny that anything is wrong. The best you can do is be nonjudgmental, tell them you're concerned and that you care about them. If their health seems in serious danger, though, you shouldn't feel bad about telling the grown-ups in your friend's life. Eating disorders can be easy to hide, and lots of people ignore them or downplay how harmful they are. So sometimes adults need that extra heads-up from people who know their kids well.

And if you're the one who might have an eating disorder, or is veering toward unhealthy habits? We realize this might be the hardest thing ever, but try to be honest with the people around you, as soon as possible. Mention how you're feeling to a parent, a school counselor, or even a friend to start. It's important to say something right away, even if you don't think you have an out-of-control disorder. It's much easier to treat this issue if it's caught early. There are doctors and therapists who are trained in these kinds of disorders who can help. There are also support groups where those who are struggling can talk to others with the same issues. You definitely don't have to go through this alone!

The All-Important Sleep!

As your kid body starts to transition to your adult body, one of the most helpful things you can do for it is get enough sleep. You probably already know that sleep restores your energy levels, but catching enough Zs also improves health in many, many other ways. Sleep prepares your brain to learn—that's why you should hit the hay early the night before a big test! Getting enough sleep is proven to boost your mood. It also makes it possible to think more clearly and prevents you from getting sick. Here are some tips for how to get good-quality sleep:

Stick to a routine. Head to bed at the same time every night. This will get your brain and body in the habit of knowing when it's time to fall into dreamland. Brush your teeth, wash your face, and try doing some gentle stretches to wind down.

Limit screentime before bed. The blue light from phones and tablets has been proven to keep you awake even after you've shut them down. A couple hours before bed, put away the devices and pull out the book you're reading or your sketchbook or journal for a calming evening activity.

Make your space comfy-cozy! Every night, slip into some soft PJs—breathable cotton ones are usually best—and fluff up your favorite pillow. Try to notice how your body feels during the night and plan accordingly. If you tend to kick off the blankets because you're too hot, turn on your fan before bed. If your feet always feel like ice pops, put on your fuzziest socks to keep them toasty warm.

Start a dream journal. This is one way to make sleeping a bit more fun. Sometimes our dreams are pretty nutty, and it can be interesting to look back on all the outrageous images your mind conjured up during the night. The trick is to write down what you remember about your dreams as soon you wake up—otherwise they tend to float away quickly. Keep your dream journal close to your bed and start scribbling first thing in the morning.

You Get Only One Body. Be Good to It!

There's a word that's been floating around lately: self-care. All it really means is being your body and mind's biggest guardian: making sure you get enough nutrition, sleep, exercise, and relaxation. That's easier said than done, of course. Some days, you will feel too busy to take a run. When you're stressed, junk food sometimes goes down easier than a nutritious meal with lots of vitamins and minerals. But when you practice self-care, it means you're putting in a little extra effort to notice what makes you feel good and what doesn't.

If "self-care" sounds like one more thing you have to worry about and work hard at, remember this: *it actually feels good* to keep your body healthy and happy. Keeping it in good shape doesn't mean having the perfect physique or comparing yourself to other girls at school and actors you see on TV, or eating nutrient-dense foods 100 percent of the time. (Remember what we said about

perfectionism? It's not worth it!) But taking care of yourself does mean tuning in to how your body feels on any given day. Sometimes saying no to certain things counts as self-care too.

In other words, if you're in the habit of looking out for yourself and your needs on a regular basis, you're already almost there. And by the way, having a sweet or salty treat is also part of self-care. It's your right—your job!—to give your body joy, not just discipline it.

ASK THE EXPERTS

When it comes to your changing body, lots of questions come up. Maybe you're wondering a bit more about things like periods, hormones, and body development. Well, we've got you covered! We sent questions from our readers to ob-gyn (obstetrician and gynecologist), Dr. Nicole Sparks.

When exactly is my period going to happen?
—Olivia R., 11, New York, USA

Your period will usually begin about two to three years after your breasts start to grow. This might happen around the age of 12 or 13. But don't worry if your period comes earlier or later than this. Some people can start their period as early as 9 or as late as 15. By age 15, most menstruating people (about 98 percent) will have had their periods. If you do not get a period by age 15, ask a parent to take you to a health care provider to assess.

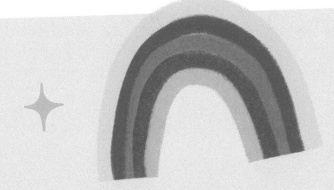

Is it normal to feel emotional and not know why?
—Emma H., 9, Tennessee, USA

Yes, it is normal to feel emotional and not know why. There are lots of changes happening with hormones in your body leading up to and during your period. Your body is developing and so is your brain, so your emotions can be all over the place. You can be crying one minute and happy the next. You may be more sensitive or cry easier than usual on certain days. Here's what can help: get plenty of sunshine and sleep. Learn some breathing exercises which will help calm your body during those times where you feel emotional. And if some days, you want to cry, then cry! Letting it out helps too. Just know that it is normal to feel a wide range of emotions during this time.

Experiencing some pain right before or during your menstrual cycle is common. More than half of menstruating people will have pain from their periods for one or two days. The pain can feel like a bad cramp in your back or lower belly. Sometimes, you may also have nausea and diarrhea. The reason for pain during your period is because your uterus (the organ that holds a fetus), contracts and releases a chemical called prostaglandins.

You can use pain relievers such as ibuprofen one or two days before your period is supposed to start to alleviate any pain. Regular exercise, a warm bath, and heating pads also help relieve discomfort. If your period pain interferes with your daily activities or causes you to miss school, it is a good idea to seek help from an ob-gyn or another health care provider to make sure that everything is okay.

I'm the only one of my friends who has started wearing a bra. Is that normal? I feel embarrassed about it.
—Isla G., 9, Rhode Island, USA

It can be tough to feel like you are different from your friends. But there are many, many girls who develop breasts around your age. The first sign of puberty is the development of breast tissue, which usually occurs between the ages of 8 and 13. There is such a wide range because everyone is different! Sometimes, if your mother developed breasts earlier than her friends that could mean the same for you. Remember, everyone grows at a different rate. So if you are wearing a bra earlier or later than your friends, it is totally okay!

**Dr. Nicole Sparks,
ob-gyn**

Let's Chat

Scan the code to listen to a conversation between our experts and girls just like you!

CHAPTER 3

I Am a Valuable Member of My Family

There's nothing quite like being part of a family.

One minute, we're bickering about who swiped the last juice box, and the next minute we're laughing hysterically at one another's jokes. I can feel angry at my mom, grateful for my dad, annoyed with my brother, and envious of my sister—all in the same hour. We get on one another's nerves, yet we rely on each other. Family can feel both tight-knit and expansive, comforting and stressful, at the same time. My family may not always agree with me. But they're my support, and they love me unconditionally.

IT'S A FAMILY AFFAIR!

All of the dizzying changes you're going through right now might be scary. But you know what can help you feel grounded and secure during this crazy time? Your family.

At its best, a family unit is a hub of unconditional love and acceptance. It's a place you can turn to for reassurance, help, or even just a lighthearted laugh when you've had a hard day at school. These are the people who will have your back, and you'll have theirs. Even the most functional families aren't going to be happy 100 percent of the time, and families almost never look the way they do on TV or in storybooks. But when you're with your family, you can feel like you belong. Family can be like breathing a huge, healthy gulp of fresh air.

Getting to Know
Your Grown-Ups—For Real

When you were a small kid, it was easy to assume that the world revolved around you. Your parents existed to take care of you, and you probably figured your teachers slept at school. But part of growing up is realizing that your parents—or grandparents or stepparents or whoever you trust and rely on—are fascinating, flawed humans with complicated lives of their own.

Depending on what kind of family you have, you might have shared all kinds of yearly celebrations, traditions, and adventures together. Younger kids often roll their eyes at these events, whining, "I'm bo-ored!" But you might start to realize now that this is exactly the time to start appreciating these gatherings and, while you're there, getting to know the members of your family in a way you never have. You're getting smarter and stronger and bigger, with lots of things to say and lots of new experiences to draw from. Believe it or not, the adults in your life probably have an idea of what you're going through and might have some wisdom to pass down.

The next time you're at a family function, take a moment to ask some questions. Chat with Grandma about what your mom or dad was like when they were a kid. Ask your aunt about how she got her writing career started. Vent to your older brother about the soccer game you lost. Ask your cousin for their lasagna recipe. Teach the younger kids a new game. These get-togethers are an opportunity to deepen the bonds you have with your family. And at a time when your confidence and resilience might be tested, it helps to hear stories from people you love about this very same time in their lives.

WHAT THE REBELS SAY

"My family and I go someplace fun for birthdays, and we open Christmas jammies on the 24th."
—Arianna C.,
10, Utah, USA

Get the Scoop From Your Family

Sometimes asking a bunch of questions to a family member you don't know all that well is easier said than done. So start with the basics!

Q&A Time: Family Edition

* Where'd you grow up, and what was the best and worst thing about it?
* What's the most interesting thing that's ever happened to you?
* What do you remember most about being my age?
* What was your favorite subject in school?
* What's the best advice you've ever received?
* When did you know you wanted to be [insert life detail here: a parent, a teacher, a swimmer, etc.]?

Mindful Break

Scan the code to learn how to create a safe space wherever you are.

Fern saw her great-grandmother Pearl at every family event, like Passover Seders and Thanksgiving. But Pearl always seemed like a mystery to her. She vaguely knew Pearl was born in Germany and came to America when she was young. But Fern had never asked her about it. Pearl always seemed a little cranky and, well . . . old.

Fern's sixth-grade class started learning about World War II, and it piqued Fern's curiosity about Pearl. Wasn't Pearl in Germany just as the Nazis began to take over Europe? Fern asked her mom if she could go visit Pearl at her assisted living residence to ask her a few questions. Her mom agreed. Pearl was 93, and her memory was fading. But when Fern asked her about her life when she was young, her words were clear as day. She was just a small girl with pigtails when the Nazis came to power, Pearl told Fern. She had to wear a Star of David pinned to her clothes. She remembered her father coming home terrified on a November night in 1938, after military men had smashed the windows of his shoe store and ransacked the place. (Fern had learned about this night in school: it was called "Kristallnacht.") That was the moment Fern's great-great-grandfather knew his family had to flee to the United States. After hearing this story, Fern was speechless. She was so glad she had come to visit her great-grandmother. Her time with Pearl not only made the stories in her history books feel more real, but it also made her feel connected to her great-grandmother in a way she never, ever had before.

Family Dinner

Some families have a classic "dinner time" where kids are peppered with questions about their days. Some kids end up crossing their arms and resisting. A conversation might go like this: "How was school?" "Fine." This brings the conversation to a screeching halt. Other kids might be talking a mile a minute about math class and soccer practice and the hilarious joke their best friend told at lunch that made everyone crack up. This might make it hard for other siblings to get a turn to share stories about their day.

Here's a suggestion: use family dinners as a way to connect with your family. When they ask you how school was, share something funny or weird that happened. Or you can create a ritual together. Maybe you go around the table and say one thing you're grateful for each day. That way, everyone gets a turn to share something. You don't have to spill your guts right there at the table—but it's a good idea to recognize that time for what it is: an everyday way to stay connected!

Family Traditions

Everyone knows about the big holidays where families gather to eat, but that's not the only way families can celebrate their bonds. Family traditions can come in all kinds of different forms. They can be religious, like attending a Jewish bar or bat mitzvah or a Christian baby's baptism. They can be based on a love for a place, like the week in August your family always spends frolicking among Lake Michigan's dunes. They can be little, everyday ways to spark connection, like having a secret handshake, baking brownies on Friday nights, or building pillow forts on Sunday mornings. Rituals and traditions can be a family's shorthand for how well they know and love one another. They can be constants in a chaotic world.

What if these sound nice, but not really something your family does? Well, it's never too late to create a tradition. When was the last time you felt really close to your family? Maybe

WHAT THE REBELS SAY

"Every Día de Muertos [Day of the Dead], my family and I make an altar, and we go to a pretty well-known fair in my hometown that sells decorations and traditional candies for that festivity."
—Mayte L, 12, Guadalajara, Mexico

it was that cozy, rainy Saturday when you all decided to play board games while listening to music. Why not suggest to your family that they do exactly that on other gloomy days too? Sometimes all it takes to start a tradition is for someone to pipe up and say, "That was so fun! Let's do it again." If your family has a super busy schedule, it may be tough to find a time when you can all be together. Maybe you can get in the habit of leaving a note for your grown-up in the bag they take to work or on the mirror in their bathroom. Even if you can't spend the whole day together, they'll know you're thinking of them.

THERE IS NO ONE KIND OF FAMILY

Some kids grow up with a mom and a dad. Others are raised by single parents, and many others' parents are divorced. And some children are brought up by people who aren't their biological parents. Instead, they live with grandparents or aunts and uncles, or with adopted parents, or in foster homes. Other kids might have two moms or two dads. The bottom line is: families aren't always formed because of blood but rather as a result of mutual love and care. And if you're lucky, you have multiple adults in your life you can depend on, whether or not they're your birth parents.

Sometimes, things happen that change the structure of a family. Divorce is a common way this can happen, and it can be painful. Parents splitting up can be confusing and feel unfair. Lots of kids think, *Is this my fault?* For the record: no, it's never, EVER a child's fault if their parents decide not to live together anymore. (Remember the part about adults being complicated and flawed?)

WHAT THE REBELS SAY

"When it came to my childhood—growing up in a single-parent home, often struggling financially—my mother definitely instilled in me and my siblings this strength, this will, to just continue to survive and succeed."
—Misty Copeland, ballerina

Hard changes like these can take some adjusting, but they can also be the start of something good. One home with fighting parents might become two, much more peaceful homes. Divorced parents may find new people they want to be with, and those new people might have kids of their own. Or one parent and their new partner might decide to have children together. What feels like a loss at first could actually bring even more love into a kid's life.

Stepparents and stepchildren are often mischaracterized in books and on TV. We all remember the "wicked stepmother" from fairy tales. But there's no reason stepmoms, stepdads, and stepkids should have a bad name. (We've also seen people in fairy tales climbing hair ladders and wearing glass footwear, and we're not rushing out to try either one of those!) In reality, though, new members of families might turn out to be close, special relationships that expand the hearts of everyone around them. Bonding with a stepmother doesn't mean that a biological mom has been replaced—it just means there are now two adults who likely have different strengths and wisdom to share.

Picture This:

Cristina would never forget the night she felt like she lost her family. Her parents sat her down and told her they were splitting up. It took her by surprise. She had heard hushed voices going back and forth at night, but she didn't think it was *that* bad! Things got harder when, a year later, her mom announced that she had a new boyfriend named Greg. Cristina didn't want a new dad. She missed the one she already had.

At first, Cristina avoided Greg, giving him one-word answers and retreating to her room when he came over. But little by little, she got to know him. One evening, she came home in a foul mood. She'd gotten a bad grade on a math test because of a few silly mistakes. When Greg came home from work, he immediately noticed Cristina at the kitchen table, sulking into a bowl of Rice Krispies. Gingerly, Greg asked her what was wrong. Cristina was tentative too. But she told him about her disappointing grade. He took her outside to shoot some hoops and told her about the time he failed a final exam in college. He was devastated, but he'd brushed himself off, hit the books, and passed the class the following semester. He offered to study with her the next day. She ended up having an awesome time. Cristina always loved math, but Greg made it even more fun—turns out she and Greg really did have some things in common!

Time passed. Greg got closer with both Cristina and her mom, and eventually, he moved in. Cristina still saw her dad every other weekend, but now there was this whole new, fun, caring person in her life. It didn't end there. A couple of years later, Greg and Cristina's mom had a baby. Cristina instantly loved her new sister, and finally realized that she didn't lose her family. It just got bigger.

DISAGREEMENTS AT HOME

We love our families, but we don't always *like* our families. Especially if you live with them, you are pretty much guaranteed to butt heads with a family member at some point. It could be something as petty as a fight over bathroom time or as serious as feeling like your parents love your brother more than they love you. (Trust us, they don't! Parental love isn't the kind of thing that's in short supply.) You might not be able to prevent these disagreements, but you can keep your head on straight before things get out of control.

Clashing with Grown-Ups

Your brain is practically designed at this age to push boundaries—how else are you going to learn and become more mature? Unfortunately, this can cause some real tension with the grown-ups who are required to protect you.

Chances are they *want* you to try new things and eventually grow into a responsible adult. It's just that it's hard to give so much independence to their baby, aka you. They worry about you, which can bring out a very strict side in some parents.

And you, who's learning how to become your own person, will start to push back!

You're at an in-between stage: you heavily rely on adults and need their permission for practically everything. But you're also at an age when the grown-ups in your life will start to take you more seriously, especially if you show them how mature you're becoming. Let's be honest, though: that's not always the easiest thing to do. Sometimes a parent laying down the law will be so frustrating and upsetting that you'll start to yell, scream, and slam doors (or you'll really, really want to). It's normal and it happens to everyone. But giving in to those feelings too often is not going to do you any favors in the long run, much less convince your parents that you're old enough to make your own decisions. (Flip back to the first chapter for some tips on how to manage your anger.)

The annoying part is that ultimately, you have to respect your parents' rules. Even if you've laid out your case about something you want to do and stayed cool, calm, and collected, your parents could still say no. Accept their judgment gracefully—no shouting or whining—even if you think they're being unfair. And if you've acted less than honorably, apologize and mean it. If you're still feeling crummy, let it out in your journal or vent to your bestie, who probably has a similar story to share. And remember: pretty soon you'll be able to make more of your own rules, but for now you have to trust that the adults in your life have your best interests at heart.

How to Ask Your Parents for Something Special

There might be some pretty hard-and-fast rules in your house. No running in the house. Keep muddy shoes off the carpet. Wash your hands before dinner. Do not use the flamethrower inside. Every house has its own rules. But even the most rigid parents find a way to compromise sometimes. If there's something you *really* want—say, to be able to go shopping at the mall even though you just got some new clothes for your birthday or to go to a sleepover on a school night—it might be possible to negotiate with your parents while also showing off your mature side. Two birds with one stone!

Start small, and make sure your request is realistic. If you're asking to have a sleepover at a brand-new friend's house, and your parents have never met her parents before, the answer will likely be a hard no. But if they know and love this friend, they'll probably be more open to it.

Find a time to talk way in advance, before you commit to doing anything out of the ordinary—not during an argument, not when you're already at your friend's house. It's best to chat during a time when you and your grown-up aren't rushing off somewhere, like after dinner instead of on the way to school and work.

Ask an open-ended question. Signal to your parents that you value their input and reasoning. Instead of "Pleeeease can I sleep over at Sarah's?," start by saying something like this: "Sarah is having a sleepover for her birthday on Tuesday. I know it's unusual, but what do you think about me going, just this once?"

Have all the information. Try to anticipate some questions your parents may have. In this case, they'll probably be curious if you have any tests at school the next day that would require you being well-rested. They may ask to confirm the timing with Sarah's mom. Give them all the details—and always, always be honest!

Be ready to compromise. If your grown-up really doesn't think this is a good idea, you have to listen to them. But you *can* ask if they're open to a compromise. In this case, maybe they can drive you over to Sarah's house for the movie and birthday cake and then pick you up right before bedtime so you're not sleeping over. Sometimes you can meet each other halfway! Other times, you might not get what you want. Like we mentioned earlier, you have to respect your parents' rules even if you don't always understand them.

Sibling Trouble

From the moment a new child comes into a family, the dynamic has changed. Your parents' attention is now split between two (or more!) kids. Lots of siblings are tight as can be, but others end up fighting . . . a lot! And sometimes, both things can be true: two sisters who love each other to the moon and back can also end up bickering constantly.

Most siblings experience some sort of jealousy or competition with each other. This is completely natural! Grown-ups don't have an infinite amount of time and attention. And siblings also often get compared by the outside world, which just makes it harder not to feel a bit of a rivalry. These conflicts can't be avoided—they will happen, and probably over and over again. Brothers and sisters are just mean to one another sometimes. What *can* help is something called **empathy**. Whenever possible, in a quiet moment when you and your sibling are in different places cooling off, try to put yourself in their shoes. This is someone you care for deeply and likely know inside and out. What can you do to make them feel safe and loved?

Picture This:

Last season, Tamra's soccer team was crushing it—they were going all the way to state championships. She was feeling pretty good about herself. In fact, she couldn't remember the last time she felt so confident and energized. But one day, during an important game with a rival school, Tamra saw something out of the corner of her eye that made her pause right in the middle of all the excitement. Her little sister, Evie, was waving a drawing she did at school in front of her mom's face, trying to get her attention. But her mom was barely paying attention as she cheered for Tamra. Tamra's heart sank. She suddenly knew why Evie had been acting out, throwing tantrums and hiding Tamra's soccer gear. The other day, Evie had stashed Tamra's cleats in her laundry basket, which made Tamra late to practice.

At that moment, on that field, Tamra started to realize that she'd been the center of attention and her sister was feeling left out. She knew that one day it would be her sister's turn, but in the meantime she could still help Evie feel important too.

The next day, Tamra set aside some time to help Evie learn how to ride a bike without her training wheels. They woke up early, and Evie took more than one spill on the grass. But then she started to get more confident. She rode for five seconds, then five more. When she finally rode her training wheel–free bike down the block, the neighbors clapped, and Tamra could tell that Evie was already feeling *a lot* better.

What Should Your Next Family Activity Be?

1. **You and your family are planning a beach vacation. Which item are you definitely packing?**

    A. A disposable camera—I love printing out pictures and making collages
    B. My snorkel, so I can explore the ocean!
    C. A bunch of books to read while relaxing on the beach

2. **It's a rainy day. How are you spending it with your family?**

    A. Probably doing some sort of arts-and-crafts project with my sister
    B. We all find a cozy reading spot around the house, then chat about our books at dinner
    C. I would pull out the board games and challenge everyone to try to beat me at Candyland.

3. **You're going to cook dinner for everyone tonight. What's your favorite part of the process?**

    A. Trying a new recipe
    B. Getting everyone involved in the cutting, chopping, and taste testing
    C. Sitting down together to eat the dish I prepared

4. **You and your cousin are picking out a summer activity. Which one are you two going for?**

    A. Tennis lessons—we've always wanted to learn!
    B. An outdoor adventure camp
    C. An art class

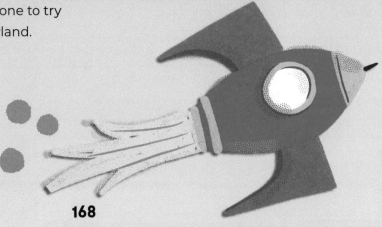

5. Your whole family is getting together for a reunion. What location do you think everyone would like best?

    A. A new city so we can explore
    B. A cabin in the woods
    C. Grandma's cozy house

6. You're shopping for gifts for your parents. What store do you go to first?

    A. A bookstore
    B. A sporting goods store
    C. I'd skip the stores and make something myself.

7. What word best describes a family dinner at your house?

    A. Interesting—someone always has a fun fact
    B. Hilarious—my dad's stories are the best
    C. Relaxing—we just like to be together at the end of a busy day

Answers

MOSTLY As: LEARN TOGETHER

You and your family are curious people. You all love learning new things. Next time everyone's free, head to a local museum, try a new sport together, or cook a new recipe.

MOSTLY Bs: ADVENTURE TIME

You and your crew are an active bunch! We suggest heading out on a hike together or trying an escape room to test your teamwork skills.

MOSTLY Cs: REST AND RELAXATION

Your family prefers quiet, cozy get-togethers. Bust out the board games and puzzles and have a family game night.

YOUR CALMING SPACE

Most of the way your home looks will probably be decided by your parents: their art, their furniture, their rugs, their books. But then, if you're lucky, you'll have a room—or a part of a room—that's your own. And you know what? It can make a huge difference in your mood if you make this space as yours as humanly possible. A place where you can go and feel totally relaxed. A place that reflects your unique and quirky personality. A place that simply makes you feel good!

But furniture and art cost money! you might be thinking. This is true. You might not be able to pick out your own bed or desk for a while. But now is your chance to be creative without needing to buy a bunch of stuff. Here are some ideas for making your space a sanctuary.

Move the furniture (or decorate it). Yeah, you probably won't be buying a brand-new dresser, but with your parents' permission, you can try pushing it underneath the window so the jewelry box on top of it catches the light just so. Or you can use it to section off a little corner of your room that's just for your pet fish or lizard. You get the idea—work with what you have! Ask a parent or an older sibling to help you rearrange your room and create nooks that make you feel happy to be there. If you hate the childish fire-engine-red color of your toy chest, drape a gauzy scarf over it. Decorate a plain wooden desk with stickers or paint. Invite over a friend to help organize your bookshelf by color.

Your walls are your canvas. Again, you'll have to convince your parents to let you do this, but a cheap and fun way to decorate a room is to concentrate on the walls. Ask your grown-up if you can buy some decals on the internet (usually pretty cheap) and arrange them in a fun way—maybe flowers or vines can grow up your wall, or birds can fly across it. To put up photos of your friends, that essay you got an A on, or posters of your favorite sports stars, get some mounting putty, which will keep both your pics and your wall paint safe. Thrift stores often have some very funky, random art for not too many dollars. You can even experiment with some peel-and-stick wallpaper in a corner—it can be tough to figure out, but you'll feel super accomplished afterward.

Make your own art. Even if you don't think of yourself as an *artist*, getting creative with your own hands is always an option. Put some art supplies like paints or canvases on your holiday wish list, or use art supplies at school during lunch. You can also put up a bulletin board to display pictures of you and your friends, movie stubs and concert tickets, even dried flowers!

Keep it organized. You don't have to keep your room absolutely spotless, but make sure it's a place that eases your stress about all the things you have to get done. Focus on creating a clean, calm space to do homework and to study. You'll feel less frazzled if your space isn't super cluttered and messy. Even if your phone already has a calendar, try to get a physical one to hang up so you can clearly see important dates and can visualize how long you have till your first day of camp. When it comes to schoolwork, experiment with highlighters, cute erasers, and colorful markers to jazz things up.

Play around with scents. A fresh or relaxing aroma can make all the difference in your room—and there's lots of ways to smell them, depending on your style and budget. Body or linen sprays are great too. There are some cheap diffusers you can buy that will turn essential oils into delicious-smelling vapor. Sachets—little cloth bags filled with dried flowers, herbs, or other naturally scented things—are easy to make and stuff into your dresser drawers with your clothes. Or keep it simple: brew a cup of tea, bring it close to your face, and breathe in the fragrant steam. Instant relaxation!

⚡ Picture This: ⚡

Esther was going to sleepaway camp for the whole summer. She was excited but also nervous. Not only was it the first time she'd be going to camp, but it would also be her first time away from home without her parents—eek! She decided to come up with ways to make herself feel comfy while being away.

She knew that smell is the sense that's most strongly linked to memory, so she made sure to pack the same body spray she always spritzes on her pillow before she goes to bed. She brought three books that have been on her bookshelf for years. Every time she feels worried about something, she rereads the books, taking comfort that she'll always know how they end. And right before she went to camp, she and her mom spent a Saturday afternoon making a scrapbook of all her photos with family and friends, so she could look at the people she loves before going to sleep.

On the first day of camp, Esther took a few extra minutes setting up her space and sprucing up her bed. She ended up loving camp so much that, when she left, she felt homesick for her bunk! So she did exactly what worked so well the first time: she made another scrapbook, this time of her time at camp and all her new friends.

HELPING OUT

Part of being a valuable member of your household is helping your grown-ups do the not-so-fun stuff around the house. We're talking tasks like doing the dishes, scrubbing the bathroom, wiping down the dining room table, and sweeping the patio.

Until recently, some of these tasks might have been invisible to you.

You were just living in a magically clean house! Or you might have been doing chores and errands since you were small. Whatever the case may be, let us let you in on a little secret: doing chores or helping out around the house without your parents asking (or nagging) you to makes some parents really happy. Like let-you-stay-up-late-and-eat-brownies happy.

Here's a Place to Start: Pick Up After Yourself

Maybe you don't have an official chore wheel in your home. But there's one thing every single kid can do to make their parents' lives easier. You can follow one shiny rule: if you make a mess, clean it up. If you take off your shoes, put them on the mat next to the door rather than leaving them in the middle of the floor. If you use a glass, bring it to the sink—every parent knows what it's like to look around and realize that all the water glasses are in various kids' rooms!

And when it comes to your room? There's a little leeway here since it's your space. But since it's still your parents' place, you should keep it tidy. Having an organized room will make you feel calmer, and we can't stress enough how happy this'll make your grown-ups. It'll also signal to them that you're getting more responsible and self-sufficient.

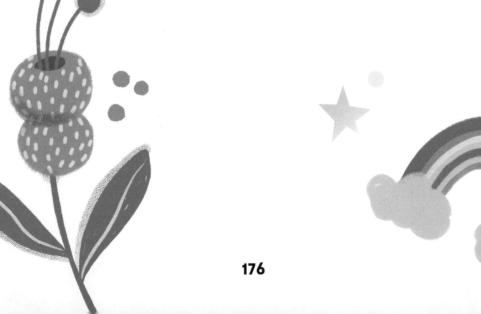

Guess What? Chores Can Be Fun!

Not everything that needs to get done around the house should be a slog. It's easy to find things that you enjoy that can also contribute to your household.

Perfect a meal and cook it once a week. Cooking can be extremely creative and fun! Your tired parents will appreciate taking a night off while you cook a meal for the family. You can start with a one-pot meal like chicken soup or a casserole. (Pro tip: learn how to use the slow cooker.) Once you master that recipe, work your way up to fancier dishes like a frittata or pasta with tomato sauce.

Garden in the backyard (or on your windowsill). One way to keep your home beautiful and alive—literally!—is to plant some flowers, trees, vegetables, or herbs and care for them lovingly. The great thing about gardening is that it can be very physical—pulling out weeds is a workout! And, by definition, it means getting your hands dirty in actual dirt, which honestly can feel like the opposite of a chore. If you have a backyard, ask your parents if you can have a corner to experiment with. Or if there's already a flourishing garden in your house, ask how you can help keep it up. No outdoor space? No problem. Herbs like basil, mint, and scallions grow beautifully in window boxes, and as a bonus, you can use them in your weekly dinner recipe.

Wash the car. In the summer months, this has got to be the hands-down most fun and refreshing chore there is. If you have a sibling, tag-team this job with them. While you're getting the car clean, you can also splash each other, cool off, and play with suds. Here's another tip: listen to your favorite singer or podcast while you work (we *might* be biased, but we love the Rebel Girls podcast!), and the time will fly by!

Caring for Animal Friends

Another great way to help out around the house is to help take care of a pet. Many dogs need to be walked several times a day—volunteer to do a few walks a week after school or on the weekends. Offering to clean the cat's litter box or feed pets will also take a chore off your parents' plates. And even just playing with or cuddling a pet is helping out.

What if you want a pet and don't have one? Though some parents will jump at the chance to add a cute animal to their household, others aren't so keen on the idea. And often the reason for their hesitance is because they worry they might be stuck doing the early-morning walks or messy bath times. Ease their fears! Look into exactly what you must do to care for this animal. How many times a day do they need food and walks? How often does their cage need cleaning or their litter box need changing? Do they need training or any other special considerations? Present to your parents a detailed plan of how you'll take care of your new pet, along with some reasons why you think it'll add joy to your life. Your parents might not be able to resist.

Of course, there are some reasons for not having a pet that are pretty set in stone, like if a family member is allergic or if you live in a building that doesn't allow pets. If that's the case, enjoy playing and caring for your friends' pets for now. You'll get lots of practice for when you're a pet owner one day.

MANAGING YOUR ALLOWANCE

If your parents give you an allowance, you're in good company! About three-quarters of American kids get a little spending money each week. An allowance is a great way to enjoy your independence, but it's also a chance to learn how to manage money—way before you have a real job. That might sound boring, but consider this: if you're smart about your allowance, you'll not only have a little cash for everyday treats, but you might also be able to buy big things you've really, truly wanted for a while. And that's a great feeling.

Here's something an adult has probably already said to you about your allowance: save some of it! It might be tempting to go shopping the instant that money is in your hand, but saving allows you to afford bigger things that your weekly allowance won't cover. Decide what to do with your money and write down your plan. Here's one option.

Save 20 percent. If you get $20 a week, put away $4 for a rainy day or a big purchase.

Give Away 10 percent. What causes are important to you? You can support them with a donation of any size. (It could be a big cause, like combating climate change, or a local cause, like supporting your town's library.)

Spend 70 percent. Take your money and enjoy! Buy a sundae with your friends, buy a book everyone's talking about, snag that pair of earrings you've been eyeing. There's nothing wrong with treating yourself.

It's such a wonderful, complex thing to be part of my family—and I'm starting to realize I'm an important part of it. I'm not a little kid anymore, so I can help make the people in my family feel loved and supported, just like they do for me. As I get older, I realize that families may not even be related by blood—they form in all kinds of ways. My family will grow and change, just like I will.

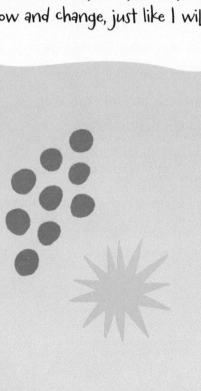

ASK THE EXPERTS

Psychotherapist Alexandra Vaccaro is back with some great advice about handling family issues.

How do I deal with anxiety about switching between two different households?
—Sloane T., 13, Washington, USA

When our life and daily routine are disrupted beyond our control, it can be so very stressful and worrisome. Having to go from living in one home to splitting your time between two different households is a big change, so it's only natural that this would cause anxiety. To help reduce those anxious feelings, start by talking to the adults in both households about how you are feeling. Create a routine that can work as best as possible for you, and keep a calendar in both homes that is clearly marked with which house you'll be in and when. If possible, go shopping with your parents and buy two of a certain items like T-shirts and sweaters you know you'll wear a lot—this way you can keep your favorite clothes at both houses and not have to worry about remembering to pack a ton of stuff when going back and forth. Being able to have some say in how your new routine will go can help calm those uncomfortable lingering thoughts.

My brother and I fight all the time, and I know it drives my parents crazy. How can we get along better?
—Kimberly W., 12, Connecticut, USA

Sibling relationships can be tough sometimes. If there is a large age gap or you just have opposite interests, trying to coexist isn't always easy. When you are both calm, try having a conversation with your brother about how you two can get along better. Try not to attack him with phrases like "you do this" and "you do that." Instead focus on how certain actions make you feel. For instance you could say: "It makes me feel frustrated when you change what I'm watching on TV without asking." Then open up the conversation for him to say how he's feeling. If you are always fighting over the same things like TV time or iPad time, try to come up with a schedule so you both have a turn. My last piece of advice would be to try and focus on things you do have in common instead of the things you don't. For example, if you both enjoy kicking around the soccer ball outside, do that more often. And remember, it may not seem like it now, but as you get older, your sibling might turn out to be one of your very best friends!

Alexandra Vaccaro, Psychotherapist

Let's Chat

Scan the code to listen to a conversation between our experts and girls just like you!

CHAPTER 4

We Are Stronger Together

We're In This Together.

Even when I am lonely, I know I am not alone. There are more than one billion girls in this world, and no matter where or how we grow up, we share so many experiences including the emotions, the weird exciting body changes, and the thrill of becoming who we want to be. Growing up is not an easy business, but being part of this sisterhood makes the tough days brighter. Putting yourself out there and making friends can be scary, but it's worth it for the belly laughs, burnt cookies, adventures, and support.

WELCOME TO THE SISTERHOOD

Just by picking up this book, you've been inducted into a club of confident, empowered girls all around the world who dream big, love hard, and, above all, support one another. Whether we're comforting our best friend when she's sad or helping out girls we've never even met, there are some qualities we all share.

We encourage each other. There's a mantra that authors and best friends Ann Friedman and Aminatou Sow often repeat: *I don't shine if you don't shine.* That means instead of giving in to your insecurities and envy, you feel genuine happiness and excitement for your friends, especially when they attempt (and accomplish!) something difficult. So be your friends' biggest cheerleader—and mean it. Confidence is contagious. If you believe in someone you love, it makes it that much easier for them to believe in themselves.

We are inclusive. One of the worst things in the entire world is being made to feel like you don't belong—because of what you look like, where you live, how you dress, or some impossible code of popularity. Rebel Girls do not accept exclusion. We welcome all kinds of people, with all kinds of experiences and backgrounds. Being around difference makes us kinder, smarter, more empathetic humans. And it makes others feel good too.

We don't judge. Part of being inclusive is accepting people for who they are. Rebel Girls don't force their own opinions on others. We respect the fantastic uniqueness of each person we meet. You may witness your friend fighting with her sister and think, *I would have never said that,* or *I would have handled that differently.* That's okay. Everyone has their own way of moving through the world.

WHAT THE REBELS SAY

"Taylor has such a beautiful way of bringing people together . . . Taylor has a way of stripping down everything and just getting down to being human. I love that."
—Selena Gomez, on one of her besties, Taylor Swift

We can be trusted. It's not always easy to be totally honest. Many of us feel shame and guilt and fear about what's going on in our lives. Enter our friends. Sometimes it really helps to talk to someone who knows us well and loves us endlessly. A Rebel Girl doesn't try to handle *every* situation herself—if things get scary, she will consult a grown-up. She will listen patiently and keep confidences. She won't take private worries and spin it into gossip. A Rebel Girl knows when to keep her friends' feelings and thoughts safe.

We're loyal and dependable. When the stresses of life really hit you, nothing feels better than knowing a friend is in your corner no matter what. Not only when they feel like it, not if they happen to remember, but *no matter what.* Growing up is hard enough without wondering whether the people in your life will support you. Make it clear to your besties: you love them, and you're there for them.

WHAT THE REBELS SAY

"I knew from when I met her I would always have her back."
—Taylor Swift, on one of her besties, Selena Gomez

Mindful Break

Scan the code to learn how to greet friends in different languages.

Celebrating Friend Appreciation Day Every Day

Okay, so, support, inclusivity, trustworthiness, loyalty, dependability, and not being judgmental are the building blocks of a solid relationship, but what are some tangible ways we can make our friends feel really special? Here are some ideas for how to let your friends know you love them.

Give your undivided attention. Did you know that scientists say there's really no such thing as multitasking? With the exception of a very few of us, humans are wired to efficiently do one task at a time. If you're thinking about the group project you have to work on while your friend is talking, you're really not being present or truly listening to your friend. Keep your eyes, ears, and mind focused on your friend when they're talking.

Be an active listener. When your friend is talking, try to tune in to not only what they're saying but their body language too. Ask them engaging questions. Read between the lines. Is your friend pretending to be in a good mood but they seem distressed under the surface? Let them know you're there for them if they want to talk about it.

Check in when they're going through something tough. A friend might confide in you about a fight with their sister or their anxiety about a crush. Offer support in the moment, but then follow up a day or two later. By doing that, you're saying to your friend, "You're on my mind, and I'm here for you."

When you think a nice thing about your friend, say it! Complimenting your friends is a great way to let them know you're their biggest fan. Of course you could let them know you love their new haircut, but you could also say you're proud of them for acing that science test or performing well at their dance recital. Showing appreciation for their skills and accomplishments is just as important as praising their style and appearance—probably more so.

Pass along a book you love to a friend. Same goes for a song you heard that you think they'd like too or a movie you're dying to watch with them. Sharing things you love and know your friend will enjoy is a wonderful way to connect.

Make handmade cards and crafts for the holidays (or just 'cause). When it comes to gift-giving time, it's always more thoughtful (and usually cheaper!) to make little presents rather than buy them. As a bonus, it can fill an afternoon with creativity that might have been otherwise spent in a mall blowing your allowance. If you're not the crafty type, consider writing a sweet card instead of buying one with ready-made text.

10 Questions to Get to Know Your Friends Better

Sometimes we *think* we know a person well and then a thoughtful, direct question opens up a whole new side of their personality. It can be thrilling and fascinating to go deeper with your friends. You'll learn so much and feel closer to them too. Try these 10 questions one-on-one or in a group!

Q&A Time: Friendship Edition

* If you could go anywhere in the world, where would it be?
* What was your biggest fear when you were younger?
* What's your biggest fear now?
* What superpower do you wish you had?
* What have you done in your life that you're most proud of?
* What's a mistake you made, and what did you learn from it?
* What's your favorite memory?
* Who do you think understands you the best?
* What do you think about when you can't sleep?
* What's something about being a grown-up that's exciting to you?

Friendships Ebb and Flow

Of course, we can't all be perfect friends. We will slip once in a while and, whether we mean to or not, hurt people around us. It's not always easy to know what to do in the moment, but being in the sisterhood means admitting when you're wrong. A big, heartfelt apology is part of being a solid, trustworthy, consistent friend.

Sometimes, there will be a disagreement that can't be solved with an apology. Your friend will think one way, and you will think another way. Or one friend will start to hang out with a different crowd and leave you feeling left out. This is when your acceptance skills come into play. It's okay to think differently. It's also okay for people to explore different social groups, seeing what feels good to them. (You know that song? *Make new friends, but keep the old . . .*) Friend love can always be expanded. As long as everyone feels respected and listened to, it can be good for people to challenge you with their perspectives.

And what should you do if you don't feel respected and happy around the people who are supposed to be your friends? Step away with your head held high. The relationships in your life won't always be smooth sailing, but they should bring more joy than stress. If you've having a tough time with a friend, close your eyes and think about that person. Do you get a warm fuzzy feeling despite your recent clashes? Or do you get an unnerving twinge in your stomach? If the feeling is more sinking stomach than warm fuzzies, you know what you have to do. It may be hard in the short term to lose someone in your life, but remember: whether you are still friends or not so much, everybody deserves kindness.

Kayla had been best friends with her neighbor Zoe since kindergarten. But once they hit middle school, things changed. Zoe started hanging out with a girl named Sophia and her friends, who wore fancy clothes and makeup. Kayla's family couldn't afford those things and, to be honest, Kayla wasn't really interested in that stuff. She missed making up silly dances with Zoe in her bedroom and swimming in the lake with her in the summer. One time, Kayla sat down at the lunch table with Zoe and her new friends. They were laughing at an inside joke she didn't get. When she asked what was so funny, one of Zoe's new friends said, "You had to be there."

Things kept getting more and more tense between Kayla and Zoe. Kayla felt abandoned, while Zoe felt like Kayla wasn't letting her spread her wings and try new things. These feelings went unspoken for months. But one day after school, Kayla suggested they talk at their favorite park bench—the same place they used to talk about their imaginary friends or joke about how annoying their brothers could be. When they sat down, Kayla gently voiced how she felt. "I feel like you don't have time for me anymore," she told Zoe. "I feel like your new friends don't like me."

For a moment, Zoe seemed irritated at Kayla, but then she softened. "I'm really glad you said something," she told Kayla. "I still want to be your friend, and I still have your back." They talked the whole way home, and by the time they got there, they agreed to set aside quality time each month by having breakfast at their favorite diner. It felt like a new page had been turned in their relationship. They were growing up. They were growing apart. And that was okay. Things wouldn't always be the same as they were when they were smaller. But they loved and accepted each other. It would be different—but that wasn't a bad thing.

BEING A GOOD TEAMMATE

If you're on a sports team or part of a group project in school, you know that everyone contributes to the overall vibe and energy of the group. Be a positive force whenever possible!

Like a true friend, a good teammate is interested in the success of other people and is genuinely happy when their teammates do well. They understand that "all boats rise with the tide." This means that when one person succeeds, it helps everyone else. They also learn how to depend on other people rather than flying solo and trying to take on too much. You know that outfielder in a baseball game who tries to catch every pop-up, no matter where they are in the field—only to crash into another player and *literally* drop the ball? You don't want to be that person. Have faith that your other teammates will take care of business. Try to share credit whenever possible. And be kind when others make mistakes.

Being part of a team is also a way to practice acceptance. Having teammates can be more like family than friendship. These aren't necessarily the friends you'd choose, but you should find a way to appreciate them. Maybe you'll have different styles of communication or contrasting ideas about what the team needs. That's fine. Try your best to be gracious and flexible. And if you lose a game or you hand in a less-than-perfect project? Eh, that's life. Not the end of the world! All you can do is know that you did your part as best you could.

Competitiveness: Is It a Good or a Bad Thing?

Being competitive can be considered a negative quality. Some people think of competitiveness as aggressive or rude, especially if you're a girl. But it can be a very good thing! It means you're challenging yourself, working hard, thinking creatively, and venturing outside of your comfort zone. Healthy competition can lead to many "wow" moments of feeling proud of your accomplishments.

Competition definitely has its downsides, though. It can put pressure on people who already have so much coming at them, and that pressure can prove to be harmful for some. It can also get in the way of a very admirable quality: humbleness. If you give in to your competitive side *too* much, there's a danger that you'll lose your perspective and start to think you're better than other people—which is a recipe for treating people poorly. Kindness is always more important than winning!

WHAT THE REBELS SAY

"At school we had to make a scale model of the lunar phases with recycled materials. While I was walking to the bathroom, I saw a friend stumble and drop her scale model. It was completely destroyed, but I helped her to rebuild as much as we could."
—Ashley B., 13, Mexico City, Mexico

Still, we can't stress enough that competition can be a great motivator for expanding just how far you can go. Which, if Rebel Girls around the world are any indication, is pretty darn far!

It can be tricky sometimes to tell what is healthy competition and what is harmful competition, so we put together some examples of both below.

Types of Competition

Healthy

* Working hard to shave off a few seconds of your swim relay time
* Challenging your friends to say the alphabet backwards (and laughing when you mess up)
* Studying for a test with a classmate by quizzing each other
* Being proud if you pushed yourself— regardless of the final outcome

Harmful

* Competing with your bestie for the attention of the same crush
* Putting someone down when they get the part in the school play you wanted
* Gloating and saying mean things to the other sports team in order to psych them out
* Being happy only if you win, even if you did your absolute best

MAKING NEW FRIENDS

A century ago, Swiss psychologist Carl Jung came up with terms to explain how different people direct and recharge their social energy: **introverts** and **extroverts** (and **ambiverts**, aka some combination of the two). How do you know which one you are? Let's walk through the definitions of each.

Introverts recharge when they're alone. If you're an introvert, you need your "me" time. You like hanging out with friends, but it tires you out. You tend to have a few close buddies rather than a big, wide network. You are often consumed with your inner thoughts and feelings—sometimes in a good way, sometimes in a bad way. You observe more than you interact. People may think of you as shy or reserved.

Extroverts thrive on human interaction and connection. You don't need as much alone time as introverts. In fact, too many hours by yourself can feel unnerving. You feel a burst of energy after a group activity or event. You love "talking it out" and immediately text a friend for advice when something important happens. People think of you as a big talker or the life of the party.

Most of us fall somewhere in between. Psychologists call these people "ambiverts." You may be mostly extroverted with introverted tendencies, or primarily introverted with some extroverted qualities. The great thing about these concepts is that one isn't better than the other—they're just different ways of relating to the world. But they *can* help you understand yourself and what you need to feel good, rather than exhausted or isolated.

Extroverts often have an easier time making friends with strangers and enjoy a big circle of support, which may make it seem, on the surface, like we all should strive to be like them. Not true! Introverts absolutely have their charms. They may have fewer friends, but the relationships can often run deeper. All that time to themselves makes introverts self-aware and thoughtful, which means they make great confidants and advice-givers. Our culture might encourage people to be as social as possible, but there's room for all kinds of people.

How to Put Yourself Out There

It's not always easy to make new friends, even if you're an extrovert. It requires a little effort and bravery. One fantastic way to do it is to get involved in activities you know you love, so you can meet others who love them too. If you've always liked art, take a painting class. Have you been ice-skating since you were tiny? Join your school's hockey team.

You could also try new things—or even start them. Having the confidence to form your own club or activity will result in friends coming to *you*.

Take a look at what your school offers, then figure out what's missing. Maybe you could start a jump-roping group in the park or organize a charity toy drive. Perhaps you'd like to host a monthly book club at your house. People are intrigued by shiny new activities. And if it's run by someone their age, even better.

Okay, but what if being such a go-getter just isn't your style? (In other words, what if you're an introvert?) Keep being your low-key self, but try to take opportunities where they come to be more social. It can be in small doses. Your alone time is important. But saying yes to invitations—even if you're nervous—can mean finding a kindred spirit with whom you can form a deep relationship. Start with smaller gatherings or make sure a trusted friend is going to be there. You got this!

Starting a Conversation

Sometimes you spot a person who you just know would "get" you. Maybe they have your favorite band printed on their T-shirt, or you overhear them tell a hilarious joke. So what do you do next? How does this person go from cool stranger to your new friend? Step one: start a conversation!

Be direct. The simplest way to break the ice is to be the outgoing one first. Say something like, "Hi! I'm Nina. We have the same lunch period—want to walk to the cafeteria together?" It can be nerve-racking to be the first to speak, but most people really appreciate it.

Give a little compliment. Chances are you've noticed something about the person that intrigues you: a funky handmade tote, an interesting answer they gave in English class, a cool hot-pink streak in their hair. Let them know!

Ask a question. It could be something simple you genuinely want the answer to, like, "Hey, do you know where to sign up to volunteer at the soup kitchen on Saturday?" Or you could ask their opinion about a shared experience, like "What was the deal with that cranky substitute teacher yesterday?"

Crack a joke. And probably not the riddle kind. A great way to get someone's attention is to make an observation about the silliness of life. Something like, "Isn't it weird how 'I'm up for it' and 'I'm down for it' mean the same thing?"

Being the Shy One at the Party

Do you feel nervous or awkward at social gatherings? Do you want to hide in the corner when everyone else is showing off their dance moves? Being shy is a somewhat different thing than being an introvert. It's not a fixed quality, meaning you might just be going through a shy phase or feel shy only in certain situations.

There *are* ways to get over your shyness if it's eroding your confidence or getting in the way of living a fun, relaxed life. You can start pushing yourself in small ways. Try ordering your own food at a restaurant if your mom usually does it for you, raising your hand in class at least once a week, or smiling and waving to that neighbor you usually avoid. Then, once you've

stretched your limits with some small steps, you can do something even gutsier: take an acting class, join the debate team, or go to a big party you would have been too nervous to attend a year earlier.

But remember, there's also nothing wrong with being shy. It just means you need a little more time to feel comfortable with people or situations you're not familiar with. In fact, being shy can shield you from being too impulsive, which can often protect you from poor decisions.

Picture This:

After an amazing sixth-grade year full of birthday parties and sleepovers, Madeline found out that her mom got a new job and the family was moving across the country. She was devastated to leave her friends and felt instantly uncomfortable in her new school. Everyone seemed to be already part of a tight-knit group, and she had no idea where she could fit in.

At first, Madeline accepted her friendless fate. Facing the cafeteria and all its cliques was so overwhelming that she started to eat in the back courtyard all by herself. But by October, sitting alone at lunch started to get really old.

When Madeline heard that the school musical was a big deal, she did a little soul-searching about what to do next. She found out the show was

Into the Woods. She didn't really like performing, but she liked creating things and being part of a team. So she decided to sign up for stage crew.

On the first day, she vibed right away with two other girls on the crew. Both were newer to the school and on the shy side. She liked their quieter senses of humor and their wry observations about the big personalities in the cast. They spent months together preparing for the play, spending late afternoons and early mornings at rehearsal, learning the intricacies of the lighting, hemming the Little Red Riding Hood costume, and making sure they got the shading on the magic beanstalk exactly right. Amazingly, opening night went off without a hitch! Madeline and her new friends became inseparable. They spent the whole night afterward giggling with pride and glee. Madeline finally found her place in her new school.

Uniquely You

If you take away one thing from this chapter, it should be this: always be yourself. There's tremendous pressure to dress and act like everyone else, and you may constantly doubt whether you measure up to everyone's expectations. It's always good to remember that you don't need to be exactly like your friends or classmates to be liked, loved, and accepted. Wear things that make you happy, and explore activities and interests that make you feel excited and confident.

Are You Totally Talkative or Quite Quiet?

1. **You're in a math tournament in which the winner has to give a victory speech. How do you feel about this?**

   A. I'd be excited to step up to the microphone and celebrate my win.
   B. I wouldn't lose on purpose, but I would feel a bit squeamish about giving a speech.
   C. No way. Public speaking is on my Not-to-Do List!

2. **You're at a friend's house with another girl you don't know so well. Do you:**

   A. Break the ice by making jokes?
   B. Suggest playing a board game while you get to know each other?
   C. Rely on your friend to include you in the conversation?

3. **During lunch period at school, your usual table is full. Where do you sit?**

   A. With some other friends I could get to know better
   B. At the table next door, so I can still talk to my buddies
   C. I'd grab one of my friends and ask if she'd sit with me at a new table.

4. **In class, do you like it when your teacher calls on you to answer questions?**

   A. Sure, especially if I know the answer!
   B. I'd prefer to raise my hand and choose when I am ready to talk.
   C. Ugh, no. I hate being put on the spot.

5. Which job would you pick?

A. Camp Director
B. Doctor
C. Librarian

6. On an airplane trip, you're sitting next to a girl your age. Do you:

A. Teach her how to make a friendship bracelet?
B. Break out a deck of cards and ask if she wants to play Go Fish?
C. Ask if she wants to watch a movie with you on your mom's tablet?

7. What's something surprising about you?

A. I can feel shy in new situations.
B. I love writing stories.
C. I want to take a stand-up comedy class.

Answers

MOSTLY As: TOTALLY TALKATIVE

You're a verbal ninja! You're comfortable commanding attention with your words. Speaking out loud helps you figure out what you're feeling!

MOSTLY Bs: PURPOSELY PRESENT

You have keen observation skills, and you use them to decide whether you want to jump into a conversation or hang back and listen.

MOSTLY Cs: QUITE QUIET

You gain insight and inspiration in the quiet moments. Your inner circle knows you can be outgoing when you want to be!

SOCIAL MEDIA AND MESSAGING

Let's face it, social media and texting are huge parts of our world, and they probably will be for a long time. It can be fun to show our personalities on the internet, and it can make it easier to keep in close touch with our friends and families. But social media can be a gigantic source of stress too. Psychologists have found that it can really hurt the mental health of middle-school-aged girls if they use it too much. You might decide that you have too many other interests (sports, reading, science experiments) to be bothered with scrolling through your phone. Refraining from downloading apps like Instagram and TikTok is always an option—and a great one. But if you do decide to dip your toe in the social media waters, here are some tips.

DO . . .

Practice the same sisterhood values you would in real life. That means being kind, trustworthy, empathetic, inclusive, and supportive. Just because you're online doesn't mean you're anonymous, and your words can hurt people.

Think before you post (or send). And then think again . . . and again. Social media doesn't *seem* like a place of permanence, but your words can definitely come back to haunt you and you don't want an impulsive statement to get you in hot water later on.

Choose positivity. The internet can bring out the worst in people. There's no reason to add any spite or meanness to the world, even if you're feeling upset. (Remember what we said to do with your anger? Let it out . . . but don't spill it on others!)

Feel free to unfollow or block anyone who makes you feel bad about yourself. Your self-esteem is a precious thing, and your feed and group chats should be a place of pleasure, not worry.

DON'T . . .

Don't go online when you're feeling out of sorts. It'll probably make you feel more disconnected. That's the time for diary-writing or venting privately to a friend—not to share or interact with the whole world.

Don't post or text super-private photos. You may not even realize they're compromising, but pics where you're not fully dressed can attract the wrong kind of attention and might even be dangerous.

Don't post any private information. That means keeping your address, phone number, and travel plans off your social media accounts, for safety reasons. If you want to tag a photo with a location, do it after you've already left.

Don't reply to messages from trolls, bullies, or strangers. They want to get a rise out of you. Don't give them what they want. Leave them on read, and again, feel free to block!

Don't tag your friends without asking. Your friends have a right to privacy too. Always ask when posting someone else's image, even if you plan on texting it.

A Word About Safety

The cool thing about being online is that you can be in touch with all kinds of new people, from all kinds of places. Unfortunately, this can also be dangerous.

First of all, remember that lots of people aren't who they say they are online. We know it's appealing to chat with new faraway friends, and that can be perfectly safe. But be wary of strangers following you or wanting to meet you in person. And if they ever ask for any personal information? Major red flag. Cut off the convo immediately!

Above all, listen to your gut. If a conversation is veering into a direction that sets off a strange feeling in your tummy, talk to an adult right away. Same goes for cyberbullying. This kind of bullying can be from someone you know or it could be from anonymous trolls, but if someone is sending you cruel or threatening messages (or if you see it happening to someone else), get help from a trusted grown-up. Do NOT worry about being a tattletale—bullies thrive on silence and intimidation. Chances are your parents are involved in some way with your internet usage already, so they'll be more than happy to help or even report the incident.

ON THE SUBJECT OF BULLYING . . .

There are a lot of different types of bullying. On TV and in movies, bullies are portrayed as the kids who hit, push, name-call, tease, threaten, and intimidate. But there's also a quieter form of bullying, one that involves exclusion, whispering, and gossiping. Bullies pick on other kids so they can feel important and powerful. If you're the person being bullied, though, it can make you feel lonely, humiliated, and sad. It's often hard to think about anything else. School (or wherever the bullying is happening) becomes miserable.

Nobody should have to put up with this treatment. So here's what to do if it's happening to you.

Ignore your bully. That's right, literally pretend they don't exist. Particularly if a bully is bothering you in public, your best option is to simply walk by as if nothing is happening, maybe even start talking to someone else while the bully is mid-sentence. If you can, simply leave the room. We realize this can seem impossible. You might be thinking, *Bullies are the loudest, most aggressive people in the world, and you want me to ignore them?* Yes, yes we do. There's nothing bullies hate more than failing to get your attention.

WHAT THE REBELS SAY

"I helped a friend who was sad and being bullied. I always try to help anyone who is sad or feels left out. Because I know how it feels."
—Aubree F., 9, New York, USA

If you must respond, keep your cool.
Sometimes there comes a time when a bully really will be hard to ignore. Maybe they're squarely in your group of friends and therefore impossible to avoid. In this case, stay calm, cool, and collected. Say something simple, like "Um, no one is laughing" or "This is boring. Don't you have anything better to do?"

Tell an adult. Without a doubt, bullies will tell you not to be a tattletale . . . or else. They'll act like seeking help from a grown-up is the worst possible thing you could do. That's ridiculous. "Tattling" and reporting a serious problem are two completely different things. If a bully physically hurts you or keeps making your life miserable even when you try to ignore them or calmly respond, it's time to tell your parents or a school counselor.

Look, we realize that hearing advice from adults about bullying can be annoying. So we asked some Rebel Girls your age what they would say to a girl who is experiencing bullying. This is what they said:

"I would tell them to stand up for themselves and that they don't deserve to take bad treatment from anybody. I would tell them that if the bullying did not stop after they tried standing up for themselves that it's best to go to talk to an adult."
—Emma H., 9, Tennessee, USA

"Stand up for what you think is right. Don't say what you think is right for them, say what you think is right for you." —Vivian M., 10, California, USA

"Bullies may say mean things, but that doesn't mean they are true."
—Leila C., 9, California, USA

What to Do If You See Bullying

One of the best ways to neutralize a bully is for another person to step in, point out their pathetic behavior, and be kind to their victim. And sometimes, that means you! Even if you're not very close to the person who's being bullied, stepping in is the right thing to do. Is a bully laughing because a girl's pants split? Offer her a sweater to tie around her waist. Do you see a bully making fun of a kid because he has a lisp? Shoot them an annoyed look and say, "That's not even a little bit funny." Not only will the bullied person be grateful to you, but you may even discourage the bully from trying the same tactics on other people. Bullies need an audience. Don't be part of it!

> **WHAT THE REBELS SAY**
>
> "There should be no space in this world for bullying, and I'm not going to tolerate it, and neither should any of you."
> —Millie Bobby Brown, actor

How Do You Know If YOU'RE the Bully?

We all feel insecure sometimes. Maybe you want to impress a new friend or fit in at school. But being unkind to other people so you can feel more powerful is never okay. Sometimes teasing is all in good fun, but constant jokes at another person's expense can veer into the bullying territory. Same thing goes with purposefully excluding others, spreading rumors, or telling another friend something your bestie told you in confidence. Pay close attention to people's reactions to your ribbing: do they seem hurt or embarrassed? If so, stop and give a heartfelt apology. Putting others down might make you feel bigger in the moment, but trust us when we say that you'll feel really bad about it later. A temporary confidence boost is never worth hurting someone else. Remember: Rebel Girls are always kind.

Someone Called Me "Bossy." What's Up With That?

Beware of the word "bossy"! All too often, a girl will be called "bossy" for speaking up, taking charge, or showing her smarts—exactly the same way a boy would. But he might be praised for being confident instead of put down for being "bossy." Don't be swayed by people who think this way. Participating and being opinionated are incredible qualities. If you have an idea or if you know the right answer in class, there's absolutely nothing wrong with expressing it. Raise your hand high and proud!

That's not to say we shouldn't be considerate of others. Being rude to people or bossing them around is never a good look. But when you get called "bossy" simply because you're confident and assertive? That's when you can feel free to ignore it—or even own it. After all, it's never too early to try out your leadership skills.

ON BEING POLITE

"Be polite." It's probably a thing you've heard from grown-ups all your life. And on the surface, it makes sense. Saying please and thank you is just good manners, right? It's great and lovely to use your napkin, not talk with your mouth full, and excuse yourself when you accidentally bump into someone. It's also basic human decency to honor other people's opinions and listen when they talk. The world can feel rushed and lonely at times, and interacting with a warm, courteous person can be a bright spot in someone's day.

So yes! Be respectful and kind. Just keep this in mind: much like "bossy," politeness is a virtue that girls are taught to follow much more than boys. And many etiquette rules are targeted more to girls' behavior, like "don't wear revealing clothes" or "don't be too loud." Girls often learn that being polite isn't just having nice manners—it also means staying quiet, avoiding confrontation, and not drawing attention to oneself.

If they concentrate on politeness too much, many girls start to put other people's needs above their own.

Pretty soon, they're bending over backward for others, even for strangers, while ignoring their own opinions or gut feelings. There are times when politeness is not as important as speaking your mind. For instance, if you have something to say in class, but someone interrupts you, it's okay to ask if you can finish your thought. It might seem easier to let the person talk over you, but this is a time to stand up for yourself in a calm way.

The same goes for speaking up when something makes you uncomfortable, when you see that something's wrong, or when you have an opinion. It's also not impolite to say no when the popular girl in your class asks to copy your math homework. It's certainly not impolite to explain an idea you have for a group science project, rather than just go along with what everyone else wants. Your opinions are valuable!

And one more thing: you don't have to say sorry for asserting your needs. Say what's on your mind respectfully, but confidently. You deserve to take up space—no apologies necessary.

WHAT THE REBELS SAY

"We can no longer let the people in power decide what hope is. Hope is not passive. Hope is not blah, blah, blah. Hope is telling the truth. Hope is taking action. And hope always comes from the people."
—Greta Thunberg, climate activist

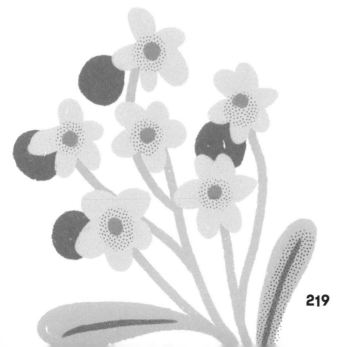

FRIEND FIGHTS: THEY'RE GONNA HAPPEN

In a friendship, there will come a time when one or both of you will lose your cool. In other words, you'll fight. You just *will*, no matter how much you love them. But that's okay! A healthy friendship doesn't mean it'll be free of conflict—it just means that, when things get hairy, you'll make an effort to make things right.

Picture This:

Soraya and Erika were inseparable best friends, and they told each other everything. One afternoon, Erika told Soraya that, a couple of years ago at her big championship soccer game, she accidentally scored in the other team's goal. She was pumping her fists on the field in front of everybody when she realized her mistake. It cost them the game, and Erika was mortified by her error. Soraya swore to Erika that her secret was safe with her—she'd never mention it again.

But weeks later, while walking to school, Soraya thoughtlessly cracked a joke about Erika's mishap in front of three older girls on the travel soccer team. Soraya looked over at Erika, who turned beet red. Soraya instantly regretted spilling the beans. Embarrassed and upset, Erika fled to the bathroom.

Soraya let Erika take some space in the moment, but after school, she caught up to Erika while walking home. "I am so, so sorry," Soraya said, looking Erika right in the eye. "Honestly, I was just trying to make those girls laugh, and I wasn't thinking at all. I really value our friendship, and I hope you can forgive me." Erika's anger didn't magically disappear, but Soraya's excuse-free apology went a long way. She told Soraya she knew she didn't mean to hurt her feelings. By the end of the week, all was forgiven.

How to Make Up with a Friend

Take a beat and think about what happened.

As you read in the last "Picture This" story, part of the
reason Erika and Soraya were able to move past Soraya's
mistake is that they took some space immediately after their fight.
Erika removed herself from the situation, and Soraya didn't just barge
into the bathroom with a sloppy apology. They both took a moment
to cool off before talking. We suggest you do the same if you're in a
disagreement with a friend. Don't send that angry text, don't sputter out a
bunch of excuses when confronted, and for the love of all the goddesses, don't
say anything in the heat of the moment that you'll regret! The sting of insults
or sweeping statements can prove really hard to overcome.

Talk it out.
After a fight, find a neutral place to calmly talk. And before
you do, think about what you're hoping to get from the conversation. Do
you want an apology? An explanation? A compromise? Ask yourself first
how you truly feel about the situation before you express your feelings to
someone else. Use "I" statements to explain why you feel let down, rather
than accusations."

If it calls for it, apologize.
And make it a good one.
People can tell when you're just spitting out apologies to
make the problem go away versus carefully thinking about
why you messed up. Soraya, for instance, unmistakably
took the blame, and even showed some insight into why

she had a momentary lapse in judgment. She didn't make an excuse, but she did make sure Erika knew that her betrayal was out of Soraya's own insecurity, not spite.

Friendship Heartbreak Is Real

Sometimes as hard as you try, friendships just . . . end. Perhaps it happens in the middle of a big fight or one sad talk, or maybe it just fades away without anyone coming out and saying it is over. Either way, friend breakups can cause some of the most intense pain there is.

Coping with this loss can be super tough, especially if you spent every possible moment with this person and then texted them constantly when you were apart. There's suddenly a *huge* hole in your day—in your life!

The but the best way out of these horrible feelings is to, well, *feel them.* Honor the fact that a friendship breakup is major and treat it accordingly. Set aside some time to just feel bad and cry. There are countless songs and movies about the heartbreak of romantic relationships ending, but not much out there about how bad it can feel to lose a friend. We see you, though. Since they're so rare, we thought we'd suggest a few songs about friend breakups (or songs that *could* be about friend breakups). Listen to them curled up on your bed, and be as sad as you need to be.

Friendship Breakup Songs

* "Bad Blood" by Taylor Swift
* "We Used to Be Friends" by the Dandy Warhols
* "Don't Speak" by No Doubt
* "Real Friends" by Camila Cabello
* "Two Ghosts" by Harry Styles
* "People You Know" by Selena Gomez

Once you have had some juicy wallowing time, grab your journal to process the relationship and what you've learned. Write down every emotion you're feeling about your former friend. Are you angry, hurt, regretful, embarrassed, relieved, at peace, or any combo of these? What were the warning signs that this friendship wasn't meant to last? Think about qualities you'll be looking for in a friend going forward and then about qualities that are total deal breakers.

We know it's hard, but our advice is to refrain from talking to friends in your same circle about this breakup. It could turn into nasty gossiping or make your friends feel like they have to take sides. (Your job, by the way, is to reassure them that taking sides isn't necessary! No matter how angry you are.) The pain of a friend breakup is best expressed with someone who doesn't know this ex-friend in the slightest—say, a camp buddy if your ex is from school. Or, maybe even better, talk to your trusted grown-ups about this. They'll surely understand what you're going through. Losing a friend has happened to everyone at some point.

"I Wish I Had What She Has"

If you end up befriending other fun, confident, intelligent girls (and who doesn't want to do that?), you may very well find yourself envying something a friend has. This might look like watching a friend effortlessly glide across the dance floor and thinking, *Why can't I dance like that?* Or it may come out as jealousy of another, awesome person that your friend seems to prefer at that moment. No matter how it shows up, these feelings can be pretty uncomfortable and put you in a funk.

First things first: go back to the first chapter of this book and learn all about how to make sure negative feelings are released but not directed *at* someone. Then, once you've gotten your strong emotions off your chest, take a moment to appreciate the friend you're feeling jealous of. You wouldn't envy this person unless they were truly amazing, right?

This is where you can transform negative feelings into positive ones. Be proud you have such good taste in friends. Remember that the reason your friend has other people vying for her attention is because she is excellent company (and that just because she's spending a lot of time with someone else, that doesn't mean she'll stop wanting to hang out with you). Be excited that you get to be around this immensely talented/hilarious/stylish/ambitious person. Remember Ann and Aminatou's "shine mantra" (*I don't shine if you don't shine*)? Turning jealousy inside out is what it's all about!

Finally, don't forget all of *your own* amazing qualities. Why else would an awesome person want to be close to you? Jealousy can easily turn into a spiral of self-criticism, so try to keep in mind all your best, most unique traits. Those don't go away no matter how envious you get!

WHAT THE REBELS SAY

"Everyone is special in their own way!"
—Lizzie G., 13, Colorado, USA

MORE THAN FRIENDS . . .

If you haven't already, you may soon start to feel an unmistakable longing for a special, irresistible person in your life. You might feel a butterfly sensation in your stomach or a squeeze in your heart when they're around (believe us, you'll sense their presence immediately). You may endlessly wonder what they're up to, act differently when you two are in the same room, marvel at how brilliant or funny they are, or become obsessed with every word they utter. You may even find it hard to eat, sleep, or concentrate because this person is on your mind constantly. This attraction may or may not involve wanting to touch or kiss them, but it usually feels quite different than just wanting to be someone's friend.

Congratulations/we're sorry: you have a crush.

Crushes can be exciting, but they can also cause some drama and confusion—especially if the object of your affection is someone you know really well. You have a couple options when you have a crush. You can simply enjoy admiring someone and feel your feelings from afar. But if you want to act on a crush? Well, that's a little more complicated . . .

Is It . . . Love?

It's safer to keep crushes to yourself, but there may come a point where you want to confess your feelings. Just know that fully acting on your feelings at your age—at any age, really—might result in some pain or confusion. If you do tell your crush how you feel, they could reject you, or they could feel the same way. It could be the start of something wonderful that lasts a long time, or something could come along to end it pretty quickly. That's the risk we all take when we dip our toes into romantic relationships: there are some strong emotions involved, and it can make you feel topsy-turvy at times!

What if the way you're feeling seems like more than a crush? Could it be *love*? Well-meaning adults may tell you it's impossible to fall in love when you're so young. But that's not true. According to experts, the still-developing teen and preteen brain is already able to feel instinctive, basic emotions like love. Still, love and infatuation might feel unmanageable right now. Your brain does not have proper control or sound judgment when you're under the spell of a crush. And since your hormones are surging, it will take a while to tell the difference between physical attraction and a true emotional connection.

So, yes, the love you may be feeling toward another person is real, important, and healthy. You feel a strong pull toward someone else, and that's amazing. But this is intense stuff. When in doubt, *slowwww* down and take stock. Write down how you feel as much as possible, and check in with yourself often. And no matter what form a relationship takes, remember this: you're a hugely valuable person who deserves respect, patience, and kindness at all times.

A Word on Sexual Orientation and Gender Identity

Around the time you start to get crushes, you may also start to get an inkling about *who* you tend to get crushes on. When you close your eyes and picture who you're attracted to or could fall in love with, is that person a boy? A girl? Both? Neither? These preferences are called your **sexual orientation**. You may have seen the abbreviation **LGBTQIA+** before. That stands for:

Lesbian: a woman who's attracted to other women

Gay: a man who's attracted to other men (women use this term sometimes too)

Bisexual: a person who's attracted to both men and women

Transgender: this is not an orientation—more like an identity, which we'll get into in a moment

Queer or Questioning: which leaves room for all kinds of other preferences and orientations

Asexual: this refers to people who love their partners romantically, but choose not to express their feelings through physical actions like kissing

Intersex: a person born with a combination of both male and female biological parts

You're at a time in your life when who you crush on or even date doesn't necessarily determine what your sexual orientation will eventually be. Some people know right away if they're gay or straight, and some people's orientations change many times throughout their life. You should definitely not feel pressure to "pick a side," now or ever! Just know that whoever you choose to love, either right now or in the future, is okay.

And while we're at it, let's talk about **gender identity**, which often gets grouped in with sexual orientation but, in reality, is a whole different thing. A lot of us are taught that gender and sex are the same—that everyone who has a penis is a boy, and everyone who has breasts and a vulva is a girl. But gender is really just a set of rules created by society about how to act, talk, and dress . . . and you don't have to follow them if you don't want to! You can be a girl and have short hair, or you can be a boy and paint your nails. Some transgender people feel that they were born in the wrong body, that their physical parts don't match up with the gender they know in their hearts that they are. And if someone is nonbinary, that means they don't feel like they're a boy *or* a girl (or they take on elements of both).

You may relate to some of these feelings, or you may not. Either way is fine, and you have plenty of time to figure out your gender identity and how you want to express it. Much like sexual orientation, gender isn't fixed, and it certainly isn't something you need to figure out right away. For now, feel free to explore the styles and behavior that you're interested in, without worrying about what label to put on it.

Just Because They're Doing It Doesn't Mean You Have To

It's possible you've spent the whole time reading this section without any idea what we're talking about. Crushes? Love? They might be the furthest thing from your mind. That's 100 percent fine too! There's no law that says you are required to have crushes, now or ever. It can be very exciting to have an object of affection, but the amount of space a crush takes up in one's brain is intense. Being free of a crush's hold can be a blessing in disguise.

Unfortunately, some people around you may not be so nice about the fact that you're going at your own pace. There will be a few loud voices who talk about crushes and kissing *a lot*, and some kids might make you feel bad about your choices. (They might say things like, "You've never had a boyfriend? *Weird!*") People might do this about other behavior too, like breaking rules about drinking alcohol or smoking. This kind of attitude is called "peer pressure," and it's not fun to be the target of it.

We get why this would cause some anxiety. There's nothing worse than someone telling you that you're behind or not normal in some way. But we're here to tell you: you *aren't* behind, and you *are* normal. Seriously, we've seen the numbers! Nowadays, young people are waiting longer to have their first relationships and sexual experiences. And even the ones boasting about their experiences might feel your same anxiety. No matter how confident people seem, most people are secretly fretting about how they measure up to everyone else. (And some people are definitely fibbing!) So if you want to take your time, you're in good company.

WHAT THE REBELS SAY

"Don't try so hard to fit in, and certainly don't try so hard to be different . . . just try hard to be you."
—Zendaya, actor

A moment of peer pressure is an excellent time to tune into that intuition of yours, which is getting stronger and stronger every day. If your gut tells you you're not ready for something, listen! And if anyone tries to put you down, you can always say something like "Isn't it great that you can do what you want, and I can do what I want? We can both make our own choices."

Consent: Making Sure Everybody Is on the Same Page

We've talked a little bit about how your body is your own and nobody has a right to touch you if you don't want to be touched. That goes double for when and if you decide to get physical with a crush. Even if you are interested in exploring, it's essential to practice *enthusiastic consent*—basically, to ensure that you're both cool with what's going on.

Let's say that you and your crush have admitted to liking each other, and you have mutually planned a first kiss after school. Yay! This is awesome. A first kiss only happens once. It might be a little awkward no matter what, but it'll go a lot smoother if you keep checking in with yourself and the other person while it's happening. Ask yourself: *Is this fun? Do I want to switch it up? Do I want to take a break?* If you want to stop, let them know. A simple "That's as far as I want to go right now" should do it.

While you're thinking about your own boundaries, make sure to also ask your partner: *How are you feeling? Are you okay with this?* This is also a time to give a compliment or a word of reassurance. Chances are your partner is feeling nervous too! Being up front with your partner shows tenderness and consideration. Bottom line? Nobody should want to kiss anyone who isn't psyched to kiss them. If someone doesn't seem to respect your limits, that's an instant red flag and a sign that you should shut things down immediately. Nobody—even someone you like—should be pushing you to do things you don't want to do!

PEER PRESSURE AND UNHEALTHY HABITS

We mentioned this briefly above, but while we're on the subject of peer pressure, let's talk a little bit about unhealthy habits you might be pressured to take part in, like drinking alcohol or smoking cigarettes or marijuana. Simply put: drugs and alcohol can do a lot of harm to the body—*especially* growing bodies like yours. As you might have learned in school, cigarettes cause serious health problems like lung cancer, and alcohol and drugs (like marijuana) can cause brain, heart, and liver issues.

Some kids think they look cool smoking or drinking, but that's usually because they're insecure in other ways.

Our best advice is to just say no and hang out with friends who are doing healthy, fun things you are interested in.

If you're still feeling pressured by people to take part in these kinds of activities, talk to your grown-up. You don't have to navigate such a tricky situation alone.

Your First School Dance

So you're going to your very first school dance—an exciting milestone, but it can also be completely nerve-racking for some. We put together some tips for you to prep for what's sure to be a fun-filled night!

What to wear: Regardless of whether the dance is casual or on the fancy side, you're gonna want to wear something that's comfortable and easy to dance in. You don't want to be adjusting your strap in a corner when everyone else is jamming to your favorite song. And even if you don't dance, you'll probably get a little sweaty. So think breathable flowy dresses, cute jumpsuits, or your favorite jeans and a new top. You can also chat with your friends about what they're wearing—it can be fun to coordinate outfits!

What about hair and makeup? Less is usually more, mostly because of that sweat we just mentioned! Feel free to spruce up your hair, just know that it'll probably come undone by the end of the night. And while a little shimmer is fine, any lip color will have to be reapplied. . . and reapplied again. Our advice? Trot out something special (a new eyeshadow, a cute hair clip), but don't get too attached to the style! And def bring some hair ties or a headband to get your hair out of your face if you get hot.

Who to go with: What pops in your head when we say "school dance"? It might depend on what your school is like. At some schools, people bring dates. At others, everyone just goes with friends. We tend to think the second option is better for your first dance. The idea of securing a date might bring unnecessary stress to an otherwise fun situation. Unless you already have someone in mind, showing up with a few of your good friends is the way to go—you're bound to have a blast with your besties.

To dance or not to dance? Honestly, dancing is a lot of fun! And it doesn't have to be hard. Just find the beat and move to it, with your feet, your hips, your arms—whatever feels right. But also, you don't *have* to dance. School dances aren't only about the music and the moves. They're also about having giggly times with your friends and sparking new bonds with that girl you barely know. So if you're feeling nervous about busting a move, skip it!

Being part of the sisterhood is like being hugged by millions of girls at once—sooo comforting, but it can also be intense! It's a big opportunity, and a big responsibility. It's important for me to be a supportive and kind friend and to spot who's a good friend to me too. Not every relationship is going to be easy, and they won't always last. But each and every time I get close to someone, I'm stretching myself and practicing how to love and respect another human. That's truly what life is all about.

ASK THE EXPERTS

Social issues like bullying and making friends can be a little sticky sometimes. Here, school counselor Beth Lucas answers questions about those topics from girls just like you.

How can I help stop bullying in my school? I really hate it!
—Ellie H., 10, California, USA

You can help stop bullying by being kind, respectful, and inclusive and encouraging others to be the same way. If you see bullying and are comfortable standing up for the victim, and it is safe to do so, step in and help. If not, it is important that you tell a trusted adult so they can support the victim and also help the bully make different choices. Remember that telling an adult about a situation involving bullying is not tattling. It is making sure that all kids feel safe and are treated with dignity and respect.

What advice do you have for dealing with a school that is very cliquey?
—Poppy L., 12, London, United Kingdom

The best advice I can give is to always be yourself. It might sound a little silly, but focus less on making friends and more on doing things you enjoy. When you do that, you'll likely meet people at those activities, and you'll be your happiest self, which will attract people to you. For instance, if you're creative and love theater or movies, take part in the school play by auditioning for a role or helping out on the stage crew. Also, as you're making connections with new people, pay attention to how they treat you and others.

Beth Lucas, school counselor

Let's Chat

Scan the code to listen to a conversation between our experts and girls just like you!

When it comes to friendships, love, and crushes, writer and advice columnist (and the author of this book!) Nona Willis Aronowitz knows her stuff. Check out her answers to questions girls sent to us.

How do you find and make friends with people who are like you—friends who aren't mean to you and will treat you nicely?
—Aliyah H., 10, Virginia, USA

There are all kinds of ways to make friends. We might bond over liking the same activities, having the same sense of humor, or having the same values. If kindness is important to you, observe potential friends first to see how they treat others: are they respectful and sweet? Do they listen and encourage people around them? Try to ease into friendships slowly, so you really get a chance to know what people are made of. Even with all this, there's no way we can know whether our friends will treat us well in the long term. Making friends is like taking any other risk: it always involves being brave, and the friendship might not always last. The important thing is to make sure your friends are on your side and showing up for you. If they're not, don't be afraid to end a friendship that makes you feel bad.

What if my crush knows I like him but doesn't acknowledge it?
—Emma H., 9, Tennessee, USA

Either your crush likes you back but is too embarrassed to say it, or your crush doesn't like you back and doesn't want to hurt your feelings. My advice is to simply enjoy having a crush instead of analyzing every little interaction. Focus on those exciting, slightly scary crush feelings (like getting butterflies whenever they're around!) while being your natural, charming, cool self. If you like to be silly, be silly around them. If you like to dance, dance around them. Show them who you really are, and if they like you back, woohoo! But if they don't, well, at least you got to have a fun crush.

If you really love someone, why do you break up?
—Ellie H., 10, California, USA

Love is wonderful and powerful! Sharing that connection is often one of the most profound things to ever happen in our lives. The sad truth is, though, it's not always enough to keep people together. Two people have to want the same things, and they need to be kind to each other. Even if you love someone to the moon and back, sometimes their priorities change, or yours do, and a future together just isn't possible. So yes, love is essential and special. But relationships need more than love to function well.

**Nona Willis Aronowitz,
author and advice columnist**

CHAPTER 5

I Can Make the World a Better Place

I Can Make a Difference.

Lately, there's been a lot of bad news. Sometimes it seems like the scary stuff—war, violence, climate issues—is all anyone talks about. But I also hear about young people doing incredible things all over the world. And I know I can be one of them. I know that I *am* one of them. I can do things to help my family, my classmates, my neighborhood, and maybe even the planet. Look out, world! I'm here, I've got a big heart and big ideas, and I'm not afraid to use them.

COPING WITH SCARY NEWS

Imagine this: a crisis happens—say, a gigantic wildfire in California—and the adults around you are glued to their phones and the TV screen. The media keeps showing images of burned houses and people who had to leave their homes in a panic. It all seems so out of control. *Who's in charge here?*

Every kid has experienced a moment like this, and it can be terrifying. But it helps to know that for every emergency, there are lots of helpers who rally together to take care of the people in trouble. Take a closer look at that news story about the wildfire. Do you see firefighters in the background? People who are handing out clothes and food? Local leaders who are offering words of comfort? It's tough to remember this in the moment, but a tragedy can sometimes bring out the best in a community. Silly differences fall away, and many people's caretaking instincts kick in.

"Horrible in itself, disaster is sometimes a door back into paradise," a writer named Rebecca Solnit once wrote. "The paradise at least in which we are who we hope to be, do the work we desire, and are each our sister's and brother's keeper." This means that in some cases, a disaster can even lead to more beauty and happiness than before. It may sound a little cheesy, but surviving an emergency sometimes helps people appreciate how precious life is.

The key to building a better world, though, is to not forget those lessons, even after the bad news passes. It's important to remember that you can be a helper too. You can set aside some of your allowance to donate to a cause you care about, like a local animal shelter. During the holidays, you can donate a toy to a toy drive for kids whose families can't afford presents. Little things like this make a big difference and will make you feel empowered.

Knowledge Is Power

Another thing you can do when something scares you is . . . learn more about it. No, seriously! Oftentimes, we are afraid of something simply because we don't understand it. Here's an example: when entrepreneur Mikaila Ulmer was four years old, she got stung by a bee *twice* in one week. The stings swelled up and hurt a lot. Mikaila was afraid to play outside. With her parents' encouragement, Mikaila started learning more about bees. She found out that they are super important to our ecosystem and that they're dying off at an alarming rate. The more she discovered, the more interested she became. Her fear started to melt away. Fast-forward to Mikaila preparing for her first business competition. All that bee research gave her an idea. She decided to sell lemonade sweetened with honey, which is made by bees! It was a huge success. Mikaila started her own business called Me & the Bees Lemonade, and a portion of the profits goes to organizations fighting to save honeybees.

Whether or not you dream of being an entrepreneur like Mikaila, you can use her experience to help face scary things in your own life. If you see a natural disaster happen on TV, why not research what causes things like hurricanes

or wildfires, and learn what we can do to prevent them? If you hear about gun violence, maybe you and your grown-ups can research organizations that are fighting for sensible gun laws— perhaps you can even attend a march together. Learning about the difficult issues and tragedies of our world won't stop them from happening overnight, but it will make you feel better knowing that there are things you can do to help.

WHAT THE REBELS SAY

"If you can't find opportunities, then create them for yourself."
—Nora Al Matrooshi, astronaut

Spotting a Fake News Story

A crucial skill today is deciphering whether news is real or fake. Literally anyone with access to the internet can publish a "news story," but that doesn't mean there's even one kernel of truth in it! Fake news isn't just confusing—it can really threaten people's health and safety. So it's super important to *think critically* about the headlines you see online.

See if other publications have reported the same thing. Have big, mainstream outlets like the *New York Times*, CBS, CNN, or the Associated Press picked up the story? Do you see a similar story on Google's newsfeed? If not, it's very likely fake news.

WHAT THE REBELS SAY

"Some of the most passionate advocates I have met have been young—because we're fighting for our future."
—Shira Strongin, disability rights advocate

Visit the site's "About" section. Does anything seem off to you? Legitimate news sources will clearly explain their philosophy, introduce you to the founders, and perhaps explain who funds them. Bogus sources will not.

Check out the design. Are there lots of aggressive pop-up ads, a weird URL, or very obvious spelling errors? That's often a sign that the site is full of clickbait or straight-up lies, not actual news you can trust.

FIGURING OUT WHAT'S IMPORTANT TO YOU

There are so many issues to care about in the world, it can make even the most level-headed among us dizzy with confusion. How do you narrow it down to a couple of causes to work on?

Sometimes the best way to start is to notice what riles you up in everyday life. Think about your daily routine and the things you wish were different. Another thing to remember is a cause doesn't necessarily have to affect your own life. Maybe you see your gay friend being made fun of after school, and that makes you want to join anti-bullying efforts or start a queer-straight alliance group.

It's also a good idea to start paying attention to the news. Yes, it can be upsetting, but it can also be fascinating. By reading just a couple of news articles every day—maybe on sites like *TIME for Kids* or BBC Newsround—you can start collecting knowledge and making sense of our big, complicated world. Click on a few headlines that catch your eye, then maybe follow a link or two within the article. You can also listen to a few minutes of your local public radio station. They often have rundowns of the daily news that you can easily digest on your way to school or ballet class.

Once you start piecing together what's happening beyond your tiny corner of the world, your passions may become a lot clearer. Let's say you're a bookworm, and one day you catch a story about how there are geographic

WHAT THE REBELS SAY

"Representation is a cause I will always stand for."
—Rayouf Alhumedhi, activist and product designer

249

areas called "book deserts." Kids who live in these areas have very limited access to libraries or bookstores. It hits you in the gut—reading a book and being transported into another universe is one of your favorite feelings ever, and you want other kids to experience that feeling too. *Voilà!* You have figured out an issue that's important to you.

⚡ Picture This: ⚡

Jaclyn grew up in a beach town in South Carolina. Some of her most comforting memories were of splashing in the waves, making sandcastles, and collecting shells for her windowsill. It had always been a quiet town, but one year, there was a big news story that called her town the "hidden gem of South Carolina." Since then, people flocked from all over to vacation there. Jaclyn noticed that her local beach was littered with garbage in the summer months. One day, she even saw a seagull eating a piece of plastic. It upset her so much that she decided to take action.

Jaclyn texted her friends her idea for a weekend beach cleanup. She told them to spread the word. The following Saturday, seven kids came and picked up five bags of garbage. That seemed like a lot to Jaclyn, until she took a picture and submitted it to the local newspaper. The next weekend, twenty people showed up! Soon, her clean-beach movement started to catch on, and there were regular cleanups every other weekend. It turned out the beautiful beach she remembered as a child was just as important to others in the community. And thanks to her, it stayed that way.

MAKE YOUR VOICE HEARD

One way to make change in your community—or even in your state or your country—is to write letters to those same news outlets you're learning so much from. Publications like hearing from readers, and many of them publish the letters they get. Did you have a strong reaction to an article? Organize your thoughts and send the publication a note! It might just amplify your opinion and reach other people like you who really care about an issue.

Another way to speak your mind is to write to elected officials, like mayors, governors, senators, or even presidents. If it seems like these adults are too busy to listen to kids, just remember that this is literally their job: to listen to the people who voted for them (and their kids!). Sometimes, writing this kind of letter can catch the attention of a person in power, especially if it's based on your experience.

Here's an example: eight-year-old Mari Copeny, also known as "Little Miss Flint," wrote President Barack Obama a letter about the water crisis happening in her hometown of Flint, Michigan. The city switched their water supply, and suddenly it was poisoned with unsafe chemicals. Mari knew writing President Obama was

a long shot, but she did it anyway, telling him that "even just a meeting from you or your wife would really lift people's spirits." He decided to come visit Mari and the people of Flint. Because of Mari's letter, the government declared a federal state of emergency in Flint, and President Obama put $100 million toward fixing the crisis. It all started with a letter, but Mari didn't stop there. Since her meeting with the president, she's organized a coat drive, started a bottled-water fund, and raised hundreds of thousands of dollars to help kids.

If writing letters isn't your thing, it's equally useful to talk to people you know about what you care about, like Jaclyn did when she started her beach cleanup initiative. Take advantage of those open-ended questions at the dinner table

253

and talk your family's ear off about the issues on your mind. (They asked for it!) Bring up your newfound knowledge of a political issue to your friends on the school bus. Raise your hand in social studies class when a historical event reminds you of something happening right now. The more practice you get talking loudly and clearly about things that need to change, the more people will start to listen!

"Even though I am small and not an excellent student, I was elected as the class monitor this year. I recognize that I don't have to be the smartest or strongest person. I can just be the person who likes to take responsibility, guide, and encourage and motivate others to do their jobs. Then I will be a leader!"
—Ngoc, 17,
Long An Province, Vietnam

Taking Action

You've spoken up and written letters . . . but it doesn't feel like quite enough for you. How do you make moves and get involved? It might be tempting to start planning trips to Washington, DC, or look into joining the Peace Corps in eight years, but our advice is to start small. Look around your own community, school, or religious institution.

Even if your town is tiny, there are likely lots of places that'd be more than happy to have your help after school or on the weekend.

What groups already exist, and what new groups can you create? Check out your local charities, soup kitchens, pantries, community gardens, and animal shelters. Do they have any volunteer hours for kids? Are there youth organizations like 4-H you can join? Joining some of these groups is not only a great way to meet people who care about the same things you do, but it's also nice to have a little structure when you're new to volunteering.

There are also smaller ways to help out in your community. Finding ways to help that play to your strengths and fit in with your daily schedule is a great way to start making a difference in your community.

Small Ways to Make a Big Difference

* Are you a whiz at math, or do you love essay-writing? See if you can tutor younger students.
* Offer to walk your elderly neighbor's dog or mow their lawn.
* If you play a musical instrument, arrange a time to play a few tunes for patients at your local hospital.
* Help prepare an easy dinner and bring it to a friend or family member who has a new baby at home.

Picture This:

Remember Madeline, who moved across the country when her mom got a new job? Even after she settled in, she didn't forget how hard it was to find new friends and strike up conversations in the cafeteria.

The memory of those lonely weeks created a new tradition in her life. She made it a point to talk to new kids at her middle school. She was able to tell which kids needed a little extra encouragement—they were the ones nervously looking around and tugging at their clothes. They were the ones taking their food and sneaking out the back door to eat alone. She saw herself in them.

At first, Madeline made it a personal mission to become their buddy and show them around. She drew a color-coded map and made copies for the new kids to help them navigate the new school. She set up weekly group get-togethers so the kids could all meet and check in with one another.

Eventually, Madeline's English teacher took notice and suggested she make it official. Madeline then formed a buddy program for new kids to connect with older students who knew their way around. Sometimes, a simple good deed can turn into something bigger!

Bringing People Together

Making people in your community happier is a wonderful thing, but there will come a time when something feels urgent and you want to do something about it *right now*. Maybe your school just implemented a dress code you disagree with, or a local bird sanctuary is about to be destroyed so condos can be built instead. This is a moment to assemble as many people as possible and make a plan. Spread the word: start text chains, post on your social media, make posters to display in your neighborhood. There's no good reason you shouldn't be the one to call a meeting at your town hall or even organize a peaceful protest. In this country, free speech rights apply to kids too.

Some schools have strict rules about protesting, so find out the consequences before organizing a rally or march. Tell at least one grown-up you trust so they can give you advice about the best way to approach the issue. But ultimately, it's up to you whether getting in a little trouble is worth fighting for a cause you believe in. It certainly has been worth it to many Rebel Girls around the world!

Change Doesn't Happen Overnight

Just because you get fired up about an issue doesn't mean that it'll get better right away. A passionate student activist is often one tiny part of a bigger movement with many moving parts. In order to make big changes, you often need adults, money, organization, lots of people behind you both in the streets and online . . . and eventually, the attention of the most powerful lawmakers in society. Those things are certainly possible, but they're not easy to make happen. And you might not move the needle on your first try. Mari was lucky that President Obama answered her letter. But even if he hadn't, that wouldn't have been a reason for her to get discouraged and stop trying.

When you're trying to create change, persistence is key.

Movements are often *years* long. In the US civil rights movement, activists fought for Black people to be treated as equal citizens. Many people think of the movement's height—when it was winning over a lot of hearts and minds—as Martin Luther King Jr.'s "I Have a Dream". He delivered this speech in front of 250,000 people in Washington, DC, in 1963. But it took a long time to get there. It was a full *eight* years before that speech when a Black woman named Rosa Parks refused to give up her seat and go to the back of the bus, sparking a bus boycott that lasted over a year. Some of the goals of the civil rights movement are *still* being fought for.

So if your first attempt at taking action doesn't quite stick, don't give up! Try, try again.

Mindful Break

Scan the code to listen to empowering mantras about being a positive force in your community.

THINKING ABOUT CAREERS: WHAT AM I REALLY, REALLY GOOD AT?

Some girls have been dreaming of being doctors or inventors or professional surfers since they were teeny-tiny. Others don't quite know, even if they're excited about the endless list of possibilities. You won't have to worry about what job you have for a long while—many grown-ups change careers a bunch of times before they find their true passions. And sometimes people find out that their passions lie outside of their jobs. There's no rush to figure out your path!

Still, it can be fun to start thinking about what you want your future to look like. Do you want to rub shoulders with global leaders? Be a boss at a big company? Spend intense, quiet days working on novels or paintings? Start your own organization that helps a lot of people? All those things are possible! Think of all the qualities that make you who you are, then try to imagine what job would fit best with those qualities. If people are always commenting that you're a good listener, perhaps you'll become a psychologist. If you're always standing up for others, that could mean you'd make a great union organizer or defense lawyer. If friends often come to you to help explain what you just learned about in science class, maybe you'll end up being a science teacher—or a scientist!

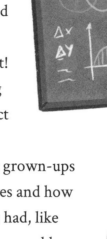

Again, no pressure to pick anything now. But it's always a good idea to collect wisdom about careers from the adults around you. Start by asking your closest grown-ups about all the jobs they've had in their lives and how they intertwine with other goals they've had, like having a family or being able to travel the world. They might surprise you with all the twists and turns their careers have taken.

WHAT THE REBELS SAY

"I want to become a powerful woman inside of a government office who has the power to make decisions. I want to work for girls' equality."
—Diksha B., 17, Banke, Nepal

How to Make a Vision Board

Vision boards are collections of pictures and quotes that inspire you. If you're feeling artsy, you could visualize your future with a corkboard and some tacks, or you can make a virtual board on a site like Pinterest. Flip through magazines or scroll through blogs and websites and save images that inspire you. These might be . . .

Positive words. Earlier, we mentioned how mantras can boost your confidence—inspirational quotes can have the same effect. Motivating and uplifting song lyrics, passages from books and speeches, and even social media captions from women you look up to are great additions to any vision board.

Real women making change. Check out news magazines and websites like *TIME* for photos of women you consider heroes. What makes them special? Why do they inspire you? Do some research. How did they get to the place they are now? Be on the lookout for women who are in careers that interest you: lawyers in suits, doctor in scrubs, or actors in fancy gowns on their way to their own movie premieres. Maybe they're making speeches, typing on laptops, or digging for fossils. These women don't have to be famous—they could be everyday people making a difference (and having fun while they're at it).

Pictures of faraway lands. Chances are you haven't yet traveled without your family, but pretty soon you might start itching to explore the world. Where would you go? What would you see? Put photos on your vision board of beaches, jungles, the pyramids, the Parthenon—anywhere that gives you a rush of excitement.

Inspo for life—right now. "The future" doesn't have to mean when you're an adult or off to college. These collages can be springboards for your next birthday party or a few changes you want to make to your personal style or a new hobby you'd like to try. Cut out pics of clothing, hairstyles, sports, activities, decorations, or just color combos that speak to you. Get creative!

What's Your Superpower?

1. **Your birthday is next month, and you get to bring a friend to something special as your gift. What do you pick?**
   A. A Broadway play
   B. The aquarium to pet the stingrays!
   C. A baking class so we can both learn something new
   D. An indoor trampoline park

2. **The school play is coming up. What would be your dream role?**
   A. Costume designer. I love making things!
   B. I want to help build the sets.
   C. I'd like to be the star of the show! I love the spotlight.
   D. Being a background dancer sounds fun

3. **It's show-and-tell at school. What do you bring in?**
   A. The latest painting I made
   B. The model solar system my dad got me
   C. The sign I made for my lemonade stand over the summer
   D. The signed jersey I have from my favorite sports star

4. **What is your favorite subject in school?**
   A. Art
   B. Math
   C. History
   D. Gym

5. What's your favorite type of reality show?

A. I love baking shows. It's amazing what people can create!
B. I really like home renovation shows.
C. Shows about people inventing things and starting businesses are so fun to me.
D. I'm a big fan of obstacle course shows or dancing competitions.

6. How would your best friend describe you if they could pick only one word?

A. Creative
B. Smart
C. Outgoing
D. Athletic

7. What do you like best about group projects?

A. Designing the poster board or PowerPoint presentation
B. Researching the topic
C. Taking the lead by delegating tasks and making sure everyone has what they need
D. Presenting to the class

Answers

MOSTLY As: AMAZING ARTIST

You're a creative spirit! Maybe you love to paint or write or dance. Whatever your medium is, your artistic energy shines through. Keep creating incredible things!

MOSTLY Bs: STEM STAR

You're clever and curious. It sounds like a career in STEM might be right up your alley. We can't wait to see what you accomplish as an engineer, doctor, or scientist.

MOSTLY Cs: READY TO LEAD

You were born to lead! You're not afraid to take charge and make things happen. Maybe you'll start your own business one day or invent something brand new. Go for it!

MOSTLY Ds: SUPER SPORTY

Looks like someone might have an Olympic dream. You're serious about sports. With your talent and drive, you're headed for stardom.

We're still young and have so much to learn. But now we're starting to figure out what makes us tick—what makes our hearts twinge and flutter. We're all so excited to get out into the world and make it better. There are tons of different ways to make our opinions known, and lots of people to tell them to, from our parents to leaders in our communities. Our confidence and bravery are infectious! And now we know how to go out and join forces with people who are just as excited to make a difference as we are.

ASK THE EXPERTS

Author and writer Nona Willis Aronowitz and school counselor Beth Lucas are back to tackle questions about current events and how you can make a difference.

Some of my friends have one specific thing they love, like drawing or dance, but I don't have that. I like a bunch of different things. Is that okay?
—Carmen R., 14, Florida, USA

Absolutely! Part of growing up is figuring out what you like and what you don't like. Fortunately, there is no deadline for figuring it all out. What is most important is that you are willing to try new things and take healthy risks. Trying new things can be scary, but there is no better way to learn about yourself and what you are capable of doing. You might be really surprised!

What should I do when I see something on the news that scares me?
—Izzy B., 12, South Dakota, USA

Just like you are mindful about what foods you eat, you should be mindful about what you watch, listen to, and read. Being aware of and learning about what goes on in the world helps us gain new perspectives and an appreciation for all kinds of people and cultures. But be sure to stick to news sites and podcasts that are geared toward kids, like BBC Newsround. If you see or read articles that are upsetting, let your grown-up know so they can help you process your feelings. And remember: it's always okay to take breaks from the news—even adults should do that!

What should I do if I feel strongly about a cause and want to help, but my friends and family don't?
—Priya N., 13, Massachusetts, USA

School is a great place to join together with other kids who feel the same way you do. There is a very good chance that other kids in your school feel passionate about the same things that you do. If a club or an organization already exists that supports the cause you are interested in, join in! If not, find a staff member who is willing to sponsor your group, and start your own. This is an excellent way to meet new people with similar interests and do something you feel is worthwhile.

You could also search for a group in your community that is working for the cause that you are interested in. For example, if you feel passionately about helping animals, see if you can volunteer at your local animal shelter. Since this might require a parent or grown-up to transport you places, you should get their permission before committing.

Beth Lucas, school counselor

Why does the news have to focus on all of the negative things instead of all the good things going on?
—Aubree F., 9, New York, USA

There are two reasons for this: one's a good reason, and one's a not-so-good reason. A major job of news outlets is to draw attention to problems in the world—this is a good thing, because when there's a spotlight on a problem, it's more likely to get solved. Unfortunately, news can also work a lot like gossip. People are much more likely to chatter about something bad and shocking than they are something positive and heartwarming. And news outlets are businesses. They want to make money, so they have to keep us talking. My advice is to tune out the gossip and focus on the solutions that can come out of bad news. The more you know, the more you can help!

**Nona Willis Aronowitz,
author and advice
columnist**

Let's Chat

Scan the code to listen to a conversation between our experts and girls just like you!

RESOURCES

Websites

A Mighty Girl | *amightygirl.com*

A Mighty Girl is the world's largest collection of media and toys for confident and courageous girls. Check out their website if you are looking for a great book, movie, music, clothing, or toy recommendation.

AMAZE | *amaze.org*

A video resource site for all your questions about bodies, sexual development, and gender. All the videos on AMAZE are medically accurate and age-appropriate.

Center for Young Women's Health | *youngwomenshealth.org*

This website provides teens resources to help improve their understanding of their own health and development.

DoSomething | *dosomething.org*

One of the largest charities dedicated to mobilizing the youth to participate in social change, DoSomething is a collective of young people who campaign for causes they care about.

Girls Health | *girlshealth.gov*

Find information about everything health-related. You'll learn everything you need to know about periods, fitness, mental health, and more, and you can also explore the site's fun quizzes and games.

Girls' Life | *girlslife.com*

A magazine and website centered around advice and entertainment guaranteed to guide you through your youth.

Go Ask Alice! | *goaskalice.columbia.edu*

Got a question about your health? Go Ask Alice! probably has the answer. Real health experts answer your questions about anything related to your health and well-being. Questions are answered weekly.

KidsHealth | *kidshealth.org/en/kids*

One of the best resources for information about your health, written and reviewed by real doctors.

RandomKid | *randomkid.org*

RandomKid is an organization that empowers kids around the world to work toward creating a better and more equitable world. This website gives practical advice and resources on how to raise money, start a non-profit, or even organize your community around a common cause.

Rookie | *rookiemag.com*

Although Rookie is no longer active, their archives remain available so you can explore this online magazine created for and by tweens and teens. Read about everything from fashion to feminism.

The Trevor Project | *thetrevorproject.org*

Provides support for LGBTQIA+ youth. If you ever need help, contact them and you'll be given confidential assistance from trained counselors.

Your Life Your Voice | *yourlifeyourvoice.org*

For anyone going through a hard time, Your Life Your Voice provides free trained counselors to help you navigate whatever issues you may be going through, from depression and anxiety to family troubles and much more.

YouTube

Just Jordyn | *youtube.com/@JustJordynLenae*

Jordyn takes you into her daily life and provides inspiring and relatable content for young girls. Watch her daily vlogs, learn about her life as an LGBTQIA+ teen, and get advice on how to find your own passions.

TED-Ed Student Talks | *youtube.com/@TEDEdStudentTalks*

Hear inspiring stories from fellow young people in this student-focused TED initiative. Learn about how students around the world are looking to improve and change society.

Books

BFF or NRF (Not Really Friends): A Girl's Guide to Happy Friendships by Jessica Speer

Friendships are not always easy, especially as we get older. Thankfully, *BFF or NRF* is here to help our social relationships be the happiest they can be. Find fun new activities to do with friends, and navigate how to handle bullies or what to do when you hear gossip.

Girls Resist!: A Guide to Activism, Leadership, and Starting a Revolution by KaeLyn Rich

Ready to fight for change, but don't know where to start? This handbook will guide you through everything you need to make a change in your community and the world, from picking a cause to planning a protest, and more.

Girls' Guide to Loving Yourself by Jenn Higgins

Everyone can do with less self-criticism. This book teaches techniques on increasing and maintaining self-love so you can overcome doubt and focus on loving yourself.

Love Your Body by Jessica Sanders

This book celebrates all the wonderful things different bodies can do and all that is perfectly imperfect about them.

Outsmarting Worry: An Older Kid's Guide to Managing Anxiety by Dawn Huebner

We all have worries . . . how do we make sure they don't overtake our lives? This book teaches coping mechanisms to make it easier to overcome our fears and not dwell on our failures.

Period by Natalie Byrne

Learn everything there is to know about periods in this illustrated guide. This book not only gives advice for every phase of a girl's life, but it also teaches the history of period care across cultures and history.

Welcome to Your Period! by Yumi Stynes

Discover the answers to all your burning questions and read advice from real girls in this funny, informative period guide.

Podcasts

10 for Tweens + Teens

Take ten minutes out of your day to listen to this podcast that will help grow your curiosity and confidence. Host Stephanie Valdez tackles all kinds of subjects like healthy eating and personal development.

The Girly Girl Podcast

A life advice podcast from a fellow teen who's been there. Carmen Applegate provides life advice, answers questions, and shares stories from her own adolescence.

Let's Be Real with Sammy Jaye

A podcast hosted by GenZ changemaker Sammy Jaye, episodes include conversations with celebrities, activists, and athletes, while discussing real-life issues, from mental health and political activism to pop culture and more.

The Puberty Podcast

Dr. Cara Natterson and Vanessa Kroll Bennett share their research and stories to help parents raise their kids. But this podcast isn't just for adults! Listen for valuable advice on how to navigate your own journey through puberty.

The Smart Girl's Podcast

This show brings to life American Girl's most popular advice series: A Smart Girl's Guide, helping tweens and teens navigate what's really happening with their emotions, mental health, friendships, and more.

This Teenage Life

This conversational podcast connects young people around the world with each other as well as the adults in their lives to discuss the issues they are facing with sensitivity and care.

INDEX

279

MEET THE CREATORS

NONA WILLIS ARONOWITZ is an acclaimed writer, editor, and author. An expert at talking to adolescents with humor and heart, she writes a biweekly advice column for *Teen Vogue* and has written for many publications, including the *New York Times*, *The Cut*, *Elle*, and *VICE*. She currently lives with her partner and daughter in New York.

CARIBAY MARQUINA is an illustrator born and raised in Mérida, Venezuela, and currently based in Buenos Aires, Argentina. As an illustrator, she highlights current fashion trends, personal experiences, and a constant nostalgia for the natural surroundings of her childhood.

MEET THE EXPERTS

Beth Lucas is a middle school counselor for the Howard County Public School System in Fulton, Maryland, where she has worked for the last 23 years. Beth serves as a member of

Beth Lucas, School Counselor

the Countywide Crisis Team and the Professional School Counselors of Howard County, is a Student Assistance Program Representative, and is one of her school's Rainbow Representatives. She earned a bachelor's degree in human development and family studies from Pennsylvania State University, a master's degree in school counseling from Loyola University Maryland, and a certificate in administration and supervision from Johns Hopkins University. Beth's favorite thing about working with adolescents is building relationships with her students and watching the tremendous growth they make from the time they enter sixth grade to when they leave upon completing eighth grade. Outside of school, Beth enjoys crafting and traveling with her husband, Rich, and daughter, Mia.

Aline Topjian, social emotional learning consultant

Aline Topjian is an SEL (social emotional learning) consultant with a master's degree in educational psychology and 10+ years of experience as a school counselor and a special educator serving children and parents from different socioeconomic, educational, and cultural backgrounds. She thrives on analyzing and scrubbing unhealthy messages from the sneaky hidden curricula in various media that unconsciously shape us all. And she can't leave a bookstore without buying a book!

Nicole Sparks, MD, FACOG, is board-certified in obstetrics and gynecology and currently practices in rural Georgia as a hospitalist.

Dr. Sparks is passionate about empowering women to take charge of their health and decreasing maternal mortality rates in the US through awareness and patient education. She is also an active blogger and lifestyle content creator at nicolealiciamd.com, where she discusses everything from balancing career and family to menstrual wellness to advocating for yourself during pregnancy and the postpartum period. She has an active social media presence both on Instagram and TikTok and serves as an advisory board member for FemHealth. Dr. Sparks is a published children's book author and has been featured in Bustle, Pop Sugar, BuzzFeed, *Glamour,* and Hello Giggles. She is also a medical reviewer for VeryWell Family.

Alexandra Vaccaro, Psychotherapist

Alexandra Vaccaro is a licensed professional counselor in the state of New Jersey. Alexandra earned her master's degree with high honors in counseling psychology from Felician University and completed her internship in outpatient therapy at Care Plus NJ, working with children, adolescents, and adults. Alexandra also obtained her 200-hour Registered Yoga Teacher (RYT) certification and Yoga Therapist certification. She incorporates yoga into therapy as an innovative approach for enhancing emotional health and wellness.

MORE FROM REBEL GIRLS

Let the stories of real-life women entertain and inspire you.
Each volume in the Good Night Stories series includes
100 tales of extraordinary women.

Check out these mini books too!
Each one contains 25 tales of talented women,
along with engaging activities.

The quirky questions in these books help curious readers explore their personalities, forecast their futures, and find common ground with extraordinary women who've come before them.

Dig deeper into the lives of these five real-life heroines with the Rebel Girls chapter book series.

Uncover the groundbreaking inventions of Ada Lovelace, one of the world's first computer programmers.

Learn the exciting business of Madam C.J. Walker, the hair care industry pioneer and first female self-made millionaire in the US.

Explore the thrilling adventures of Junko Tabei, the first female climber to summit Mount Everest.

Discover the inspiring story of Dr. Wangari Maathai, the Nobel Peace Prize–winning environmental activist from Kenya.

Follow the awe-inspiring career of Alicia Alonso, a world-renowned prima ballerina from Cuba.

REBEL GIRLS App®

LISTEN TO MORE EMPOWERING STORIES ON THE REBEL GIRLS APP

Download the app to listen to beloved Rebel Girls stories, as well as brand-new tales of extraordinary women. Filled with the adventures and accomplishments of women from around the world and throughout history, the Rebel Girls app is designed to entertain, inspire, and build confidence in listeners everywhere.

Plus, find QR codes throughout this book that unlock unforgettable audio content!

ABOUT REBEL GIRLS

REBEL GIRLS is a global, multi-platform empowerment brand dedicated to helping raise the most inspired and confident generation of girls through content, experiences, products, and community. Originating from an international best-selling children's book, Rebel Girls amplifies stories of real-life women throughout history, geography, and field of excellence. With a growing community of nearly 20 million self-identified Rebel Girls spanning more than 100 countries, the brand engages with Generation Alpha through its book series, award-winning podcast, events, and merchandise. With the 2021 launch of the Rebel Girls app, the company has created a flagship destination for girls to explore a wondrous world filled with inspiring true stories of extraordinary women.

As a B corp, we're part of a global community of businesses that meets high standards of social and environmental impact.

Join the Rebel Girls community:
- ✦ Facebook: facebook.com/rebelgirls
- ✦ Instagram: @rebelgirls
- ✦ Twitter: @rebelgirlsbook
- ✦ TikTok: @rebelgirlsbook
- ✦ Web: rebelgirls.com
- ✦ Podcast: rebelgirls.com/podcast
- ✦ App: rebelgirls.com/app

If you liked this book, please take a moment to review it wherever you prefer!